D0429147

THE DALAI LAMA'S
LITTLE BOOK OF WISDOM

The

DALAI LAMA'S

Little Book of

WISDOM

BARNES
&NOBLE
BOOKS
NEW YORK

This edition published by BARNES & NOBLE INC.
By arrangement with THORSONS
An Imprint of HarperCollins*Publishers*

2002 BARNES & NOBLE BOOKS

3 5 7 9 10 8 6 4

© His Holiness the Dalai Lama 1995, 1997, 2000

His Holiness the Dalai Lama asserts the moral right to be
identified as the author of this work.

Buddha motif by Rochelle Green

Text derived from *The Power of Compassion*,
The Four Noble Truths, *Transforming the Mind*
published by Thorsons

Previously published by Thorsons as separate volumes:
The Dalai Lama's Book of Wisdom
The Dalai Lama's Book of Transformation
The Dalai Lama's Book of Love and Compassion

A catalogue record for this book is
available from the British Library

ISBN 0-7607-3739-8

Printed and bound in Thailand by Imago

All rights reserved. No part of this publication may be
reproduced, stored in a retrieval system, or transmitted,
in any form or by any means, electronic, mechanical,
photocopying, recording or otherwise, without the prior
permission of the publishers.

~

CONTENTS

~

~

FOREWORD

The Dalai Lama's Little Book of Wisdom is a collection of teachings given by His Holiness the Dalai Lama in a series of talks, lectures and question and answer sessions in the UK during 1993, 1996 and 1999.

His Holiness the Dalai Lama is the spiritual and temporal leader of the Tibetan people. In 1989 His Holiness the Dalai Lama was awarded the Nobel Peace Prize for his non-violent struggle for the liberation of Tibet. Since 1959 His Holiness has been living in exile in India. Tibet continues to be occupied by Communist China.

~

It is hoped that *The Dalai Lama's Little Book of Wisdom* will bring His Holiness the Dalai Lama's message about the importance of love, compassion, forgiveness, balanced attitudes and positive thinking to a wider audience.

The Office of Tibet would like to thank Jane Rasch and Cait Collins for transcribing His Holiness the Dalai Lama's talks and lectures, and Dr Thupten Jinpa and Dominique Side for interpreting and editing His Holiness' teachings into English.

~

PREFACE

I am a Buddhist and my whole way of training is according to the Buddhist teaching or Buddha *Dharma*. Although I speak from my own experience, I feel that no one has the right to impose his or her beliefs on another person. I will not propose to you that my way is best. The decision is up to you. If you find some point which may be suitable for you, then you can carry out experiments for yourself. If you find that it is of no use, then you can discard it.

His Holiness the XIV Dalai Lama

PART ONE

CONTENTMENT, JOY
AND LIVING WELL

~

The basic fact is that all sentient beings, particularly human beings, want happiness and do not want pain and suffering. On those grounds, we have every right to be happy and to use different methods or means to overcome suffering and to achieve happier lives. It is worthwhile to think seriously about the positive and negative consequences of these methods. You should be aware that there are differences between short-term interest and long-term interest and consequences – and the long-term interest is more important. Buddhists usually say that there is no absolute and that everything is relative. So we must judge according to the circumstances.

~

Our experiences and feelings are mainly related to our bodies and our minds. We know from our daily experience that mental happiness is beneficial. For instance, though two people may face the same kind of tragedy, one person may face it more easily than the other due to his or her mental attitude.

~

~

I believe that if someone really wants a happy life then it is very important to pursue both internal and external means; in other words, mental development and material development. One could also say 'spiritual development', but when I say 'spiritual' I do not necessarily mean any kind of religious faith. When I use the word 'spiritual' I mean basic human good qualities. These are: human affection, a sense of involvement, honesty, discipline and human intelligence properly guided by good motivation. We have all these qualities from birth; they do not come to us later in our lives.

~

~

As humans, we all have the same human potential, unless there is some sort of retarded brain function. The wonderful human brain is the source of our strength and the source of our future, provided we utilize it in the right direction. If we use the brilliant human mind in the wrong way, it is really a disaster.

~

~

I think human beings are the superior sentient beings on this planet. Humans have the potential not only to create happy lives for themselves, but also to help other beings. We have a natural creative ability and it is very important to realize this.

~

~

With the realization of one's own potential and self-confidence in one's ability, one can build a better world. According to my own experience, self-confidence is very important. That sort of confidence is not a blind one; it is an awareness of one's own potential. On that basis, human beings can transform themselves by increasing the good qualities and reducing the negative qualities.

~

~

The fundamental teaching of the Buddha is his teaching on the Four Noble Truths: 1) That there is suffering; 2) that suffering has cause; 3) that there is cessationof suffering; and, 4) that there is a path to suchfreedom. The underlying principle of this teaching is the universal principle of causality. What becomes important in the understanding of this basic teaching is a genuine awareness of one's own potentials and the need to utilize them to their fullest. Seen in this light, every human action becomes significant.

~

~

It is my belief that the human brain and basic human compassion are by nature in some kind of balance. Sometimes, when we grow up, we may neglect human affection and simply concentrate on the human brain, thus losing the balance. It is then that disasters and unwelcome things happen.

~

~

The smile is a very important feature of the human face. But because of human intelligence, even that good part of human nature can be used in the wrong way, such as sarcastic smiles or diplomatic smiles, which only serve to create suspicion. I feel that a genuine, affectionate smile is very important in our day-to-day lives. How one creates that smile largely depends on one's own attitude. It is illogical to expect smiles from others if one does not smile oneself. Therefore, one can see that many things depend on one's own behaviour.

~

~

The important thing is to use human intelligence and judgement, and to be mindful of the benefits for long-term and short-term happiness. Up to a certain point, the body itself is a good indicator. For instance, if some sort of food causes you discomfort one day, then later you will not want to consume that type of food. It seems that at a certain stage the body itself can tell us what is suitable for well-being and happiness and what is not.

~

~

Sometimes your intelligence may oppose your immediate desire because it knows the long-term consequences. Thus, the role of intelligence is to determine the positive and negative potential of an event or factor which could have both positive and negative results. It is the role of intelligence, with the full awareness that is provided by education, to judge and accordingly utilize the potential for one's own benefit or well-being.

~

~

If we examine our mental world, we find that there are various mental factors which have both positive and negative aspects. For instance, we can look at two types which are quite similar: one is self-confidence and the other is conceit or pride. Both of them are similar in that they are uplifting states of mind which give you a certain degree of confidence and boldness. But conceit and pride tend to lead to more negative consequences, whereas self-confidence tends to lead to more positive consequences.

~

~

I usually make a distinction between different types of ego. One type of ego is self-cherishing in order to get some benefit for itself, disregarding the rights of others. This is the negative ego. Another ego says, 'I must be a good human being. I must serve. I must take full responsibility.' That kind of strong feeling of 'I' or self opposes some of our negative emotions.

~

~

So there are two types of ego, and wisdom or intelligence makes a distinction. Similarly, we must be able to distinguish between genuine humility and a lack of confidence. One may mistake the two because both of these are sort of slightly humbling mental functions, but one is positive and the other is negative.

~

~

There is both positive and negative desire. For instance, the Mahayana Buddhist literature mentions two desires or two aspirations. One is the aspiration to be of benefit to all sentient beings and the other is the aspiration to attain fully the Enlightened state for that purpose. Without these two types of aspiration, the attainment of full Enlightenment is impossible. But there are also negative things which result from desire. The antidote to this negative desire is contentment. There are always extremes, but the middle way is the proper way.

~

~

The sense of contentment is a key factor for attaining happiness. Bodily health, material wealth and companions and friends are three factors for happiness. Contentment is the key that will determine the outcome of your relations with all three of these factors.

~

~

When our attitude towards our material possessions and wealth is not proper, it can lead to an extreme attachment towards such things as our property, houses and belongings. This can lead to an inability to feel contented. If that happens, then one will always remain in a state of dissatisfaction, always wanting more. In a way, one is then really poor, because the suffering of poverty is the suffering of wanting something and feeling the lack of it.

~

Now when we talk about objects of enjoyment or desire and material well-being, Buddhist literature mentions five types of objects of desire: form, sound, odours, tastes and tactile sensations. Whether or not these objects of enjoyment give rise to happiness, satisfaction and contentment, or conversely, give rise to suffering and dissatisfaction depends very much on how you apply your faculty of intelligence. Our behaviour in our daily lives is the key factor in determining whether these really produce genuine, long-lasting satisfaction or not. Much depends on our own attitude. And for this mental factor, motivation is the key thing.

In Buddhist literature, human life is seen as a favourable form of existence or rebirth. There are various factors that could complement the favourable existence as a human being, such as having a long life, good health, material possessions and eloquence so that one can relate to others in a more beneficial way. But whether or not these conditions lead to a more beneficial existence or a more harmful one depends very much on how you utilize them and whether or not you apply the faculty of intelligence.

~

Buddhist literature mentions practice of the Six Perfections. For instance, in the case of acquiring ma-terial possessions, according to Buddhism, generosity and the act of giving are seen as causes of wealth. But in order to practise generosity and giving successfully, one must first of all have a sound ethical discipline. And that ethical discipline can come about only if one has the ability to bear hardships when confronted with them. For that you also need a certain degree of joyful effort.

~

~

In order to practise the application of joyful effort successfully, one must have the ability to concentrate, to focus on events, actions or goals. That in turn depends on whether or not you have the ability to exercise your power of judgement, to judge between what is desirable and what is undesirable, what is negative and what is positive.

~

～

How do we go about implementing in our daily lives the principles which are stipulated in the practice of the Six Perfections? Buddhism recommends living one's life within the ethical discipline of observance of what are known as the Ten Precepts, or Avoidance of the Ten Negative Actions. Most of the Negative Actions are common denominators of all religious traditions. They are seen as negative or undesirable for society in general, regardless of any religious point of view.

～

~

Good conduct is the way in which life becomes more meaningful, more constructive and more peaceful. For this, much depends on our own behaviour and our mental attitude.

~

PART TWO

FACING DEATH
AND DYING

~

The issue of facing death in a peaceful manner is a very difficult one. According to common sense, there seem to be two ways of dealing with the problem and the suffering. The first is simply to try to avoid the problem, to put it out of your mind, even though the reality of that problem is still there and it is not minimized. Another way of dealing with this issue is to look directly at the problem and analyse it, make it familiar to you and make it clear that it is a part of all our lives.

~

~

Illness happens. It is not something exceptional; it is part of nature and a fact of life. Of course we have every right to avoid illness and pain, but in spite of that effort, when illness happens it is better to accept it. While you should make every effort to cure it as soon as possible, you should have no extra mental burden. As the great Indian scholar Shantideva has said: 'If there is a way to overcome the suffering, then there is no need to worry; if there is no way to overcome the suffering, then there is no use in worrying.' That kind of rational attitude is quite useful.

~

~

Death is a part of all our lives. Whether we like it or not, it is bound to happen. Instead of avoiding thinking about it, it is better to understand its meaning. We all have the same body, the same human flesh, and therefore we will all die. There is a big difference, of course, between natural death and accidental death, but basically death will come sooner or later. If from the beginning your attitude is, 'Yes, death is part of our lives', then it may be easier to face.

~

There are two distinct approaches to dealing with a problem. One is to simply avoid it by not thinking about it. The other, which is much more effective, is to face it directly so that you are already conscious of it. Generally there are two types of problem or suffering: with one type, it is possible that, by adopting a certain attitude, one will be able to actually reduce the force and level of suffering and anxiety. However, there could be other types of problems and suffering for which adopting a certain type of attitude and way of thinking may not necessarily reduce the level of suffering, but which would still prepare you to face it.

~

When unfortunate things happen in our lives there are two possible results. One possibility is mental unrest, anxiety, fear, doubt, frustration and eventually depression, and, in the worst case, even suicide. That's one way. The other possibility is that because of that tragic experience you become more realistic, you become closer to reality. With the power of investigation, the tragic experience may make you stronger and increase your self-confidence and self-reliance. The unfortunate event can be a source of inner strength.

~

~

The success of our lives and our future depends on our motivation and determination or self-confidence. Through difficult experiences, life sometimes becomes more meaningful. If you look at people who, from the beginning of their lives, have had everything, you may see that when small things happen they soon lose hope or grow irritated. Others have developed stronger mental attitudes as a result of their hardships.

~

~

I think the person who has had more experience of hardships can stand more firmly in the face ofproblems than the person who has never experienced suffering. From this angle then, some suffering can be a good lesson for life.

~

~

Personally, I have lost my country and, worse still, in my country there has been a lot of destruction, suffering and unhappiness. I have spent not only the majority of my life but also the best part of my life outside Tibet. If you think of this from that angle alone, there is hardly anything that is positive. But from another angle, you can see that because of these unfortunate things I have had another type of freedom, such as the opportunity of meeting different people from different traditions and also of meeting scientists from different fields. From those experiences my life has been enriched and I have learned many valuable things. So my tragic experiences have also had some valuable aspects.

~

Looking at problems from different angles actually lessens the mental burden. From the Buddhist viewpoint, every event has many aspects and naturally one event can be viewed from many, many different angles. It is very rare or almost impossible that an event can be negative from all points of view. Therefore, it is useful when something happens to try to look at it from different angles and then you can see the positive or beneficial aspects. Moreover, if something happens, it is very useful immediately to make a comparison with some other event or with the events of other people or other nations. This is also very helpful in sustaining your peace of mind.

~

~

I will now explain, as a Buddhist monk, how to deal with death. Buddha taught the principles of the Four Noble Truths, the first of which is the Truth of Suffering. The Truth of Suffering is taught within the context of three characteristics of existence, the first being impermanence. When talking about the nature of impermanence we must bear in mind that there are two levels. One is the coarse level, which is quite obvious and is the cessation of the continuation of a life or an event. But the impermanent nature which is being taught in relation to the Four Noble Truths refers to the more subtle aspect of impermanence, which is the transitory nature of existence.

~

By reflecting on the coarser levels of impermanence one will be able to confront and counteract grasping at permanence or eternal existence of one's own identity or self, because it is grasping at permanence that forces us to cling onto this very 'now-ness' or matters of one's lifetime alone. By releasing the grip of this grasping and enduring within us, we will be in a better position to appreciate the value of working for our future lifetimes.

~

~

One of the reasons why awareness of death and impermanence is so crucial in the Buddhist religious practice is that it is considered that your state of mind at the time of death has a very great effect on determining what form of rebirth you might take. Whether it is a positive state of mind or a negative one will have a great effect. Therefore, Buddhist religious practice greatly emphasizes the importance of the awareness of death and impermanence.

~

~

One of the positive side-effects of maintaining a very high degree of awareness of death is that it will prepare the individual to such an extent that, when the individual actually faces death, he or she will be in a better position to maintain his or her presence of mind. Especially in Tantric Buddhism, it is considered that the state of mind which one experiences at the point of death is extremely subtle and, because of the subtlety of the level of that consciousness, it also has a great power and impact upon one's mental continuum.

~

~

In Tantric practices we find a lot of emphasis placed on reflections upon the process of death, so that the individual at the time of death not only retains his or her presence of mind, but also is in a position to utilize that subtle state of consciousness effectively towards the realization of the path.

~

~

From the Tantric perspective, the entire process of
existence is explained in terms of the three stages
known as 'death', the 'intermediate state' and
'rebirth'. All of these three stages of existence are
seen as states or manifestations of the consciousness and the energies that accompany or propel
the consciousness, so that the intermediate state
and rebirth are nothing other than various levels of
the subtle consciousness and energy. An example
of such fluctuating states can be found in our daily
existence, when during the 24-hour day we go
through a cycle of deep sleep, the waking period
and the dream state. Our daily existence is in fact
characterized by these three stages.

~

As death becomes something familiar to you, as you have some knowledge of its processes and can recognize its external and internal indications, you are prepared for it. According to my own experience, I still have no confidence that at the moment of death I will really implement all these practices for which I have prepared. I have no guarantee!

~

~

Sometimes when I think about death I get some kind of excitement. Instead of fear, I have a feeling of curiosity and this makes it much easier for me to accept death. Of course, my only burden if I die today is, 'Oh, what will happen to Tibet? What about Tibetan culture? What about the six million Tibetan people's rights?' This is my main concern. Otherwise, I feel almost no fear of death.

~

~

In my daily practice of prayer I visualize eight different deity yogas and eight different deaths. Perhaps when death comes all my preparation may fail. I hope not! I think these practices are mentally very helpful in dealing with death. Even if there is no next life, there is some benefit if they relieve fear. And because there is less fear, one can be more fully prepared. If you are fully prepared then, at the moment of death, you can retain your peace of mind.

~

~

I think at the time of death a peaceful mind is essential no matter what you believe in, whether it is Buddhism or some other religion. At the moment of death, the individual should not seek to develop anger, hatred and so on. I think even non-believers see that it is better to pass away in a peaceful manner, it is much happier. Also, for those who believe in heaven or some other concept, it is also best to pass away peacefully with the thought of one's own God or belief in higher forces. For Buddhists and also other ancient Indian traditions, which accept the rebirth or karma theory, naturally at the time of death a virtuous state of mind is beneficial.

PART THREE

DEALING WITH
ANGER AND EMOTION

~

Anger and hatred are two of our closest friends. When I was young I had quite a close relationship with anger. Then eventually I found a lot of disagreement with anger. By using common sense, with the help of compassion and wisdom, I now have a more powerful argument with which to defeat anger.

~

~

Perhaps there are two types of anger. One type of anger could be transformed into a positive emotion. For example, if one has a sincere compassionate motivation and concern for someone and that person does not heed one's warning about his or her actions, then there is no alternative except the use of some kind of force to stop that person's misdeeds.

~

~

According to my experience, it is clear that if each individual makes an effort then he or she can change. Of course, change is not immediate and it takes a lot of time. In order to change and deal with emotions it is crucial to analyse which thoughts are useful, constructive and of benefit to us. I mean mainly those thoughts which make us calmer, more relaxed and which give us peace of mind, versus those thoughts which create uneasiness, fear and frustration.

~

Within the body there are billions of different particles. Similarly, there are many different thoughts and a variety of states of mind. It is wise to take a close look into the world of your mind and to make the distinction between beneficial and harmful states of mind. Once you can recognize the value of good states of mind, you can increase or foster them.

Buddha taught the principles of the Four Noble Truths and these form the foundation of the Buddha *Dharma*. The Third Noble Truth is cessation. In this context cessation means the state of mind or mental quality which, through practice and effort, ceases all the negative emotions. It is a state in which the individual has reached a perfected state of mind which is free from the effects of various afflictive and negative emotions and thoughts.

The state of true cessation is, according to Buddhism, the refuge that all practising Buddhists seek. The reason one seeks refuge in the Buddha, is not because Buddha was from the beginning a special person, but because Buddha realized the state of true cessation.

~

Generally speaking, in Buddhist literature, a negative emotion or thought is defined as 'a state which causes disturbance within one's mind'. These afflictive emotions and thoughts are factors that create unhappiness and turmoil within us. Emotion in general is not necessarily something negative. At a scientific conference which I attended along with many psychologists and neuro-scientists, it was concluded that even Buddhas have emotion, according to the definition of emotion found in various scientific disciplines. So *karuna* (infinite compassion or kindness) can be described as a kind of emotion.

~

~

Naturally emotions can be positive and negative. However, when talking about anger, etc., we are deal-ing with negative emotions. Negative emotions are those which immediately create some kind of unhappiness or uneasiness and which, in the long run, create certain actions. Those actions ultimately lead to harm to others and this brings pain or suffering to oneself. This is what we mean by negative emotions.

~

In Tantric practice there are meditative techniques which enable the transformation of the energy of anger. This is the reason behind the wrathful deities. On the basis of compassionate motivation, anger may in some cases be useful because it gives us extra energy and enables us to act swiftly. However, anger usually leads to hatred and hatred is always negative. Hatred harbours ill will.

~

I usually analyse anger on two levels: on the basic human level and on the Buddhist level. From the human level, without any reference to a religious tradition or ideology, we can look at the sources of our happiness: good health, material facilities and good companions. Now from the stand-point of health, negative emotions such as hatred are very bad.

~

~

Your mental state should always remain calm. Even if some anxiety occurs, as it is bound to in life, you should always be calm. Like a wave, which rises from the water and dissolves back into the water, these disturbances are very short, so they should not affect your basic mental attitude. If you remain calm your blood pressure and so on remains more normal and as a result your health will improve.

~

~

Some of my close friends have high blood pressure, yet they never come near to having crises in their health and they never feel tired. Over the years I have met some very good practitioners. Meanwhile, there are other friends who have great material comfort yet, when we start to talk, after the initial few nice words, they begin to complain and grieve. In spite of their material prosperity, these people do not have calm or peaceful minds. As a result, they are always wor-rying about their digestion, their sleep, everything! Therefore it is clear that mental calmness is a very important factor for good health.

~

The second source of happiness comes from our ma-terial facilities. Sometimes when I wake up in the early morning, if my mood is not very good, then when I look at my watch I feel uncomfortable because of my mood. Then on other days, due perhaps to the previous day's experience, when I wake up my mood is pleasant and peaceful. At that time, when I look at my watch I see it as extraordinarily beautiful. Yet it is the same watch, isn't it? The difference comes from mental attitude. Whether our use of our material facilities provides genuine satisfaction or not depends on our mental attitude.

~

It is bad for our material possessions if our mind is dominated by anger. To speak again from my own experience, when I was young I sometimes repaired watches. I tried and failed many times. Sometimes I would lose my patience and hit the watch! During those moments, my anger altered my whole attitude and afterwards I felt very sorry for my actions. If my goal was to repair the watch, then why did I hit it on the table? Again you can see how one's mental attitude is crucial in order to utilize material facilities for one's own genuine satisfaction or benefit.

~

~

The third source of happiness is our companions. It is obvious that when you are mentally calm you are honest and open-minded. Even if there is a big difference of opinion, you can communicate on a human level. You can put aside these different opinions and communicate as human beings. I think that is one way to create positive feelings in other people's minds.

~

~

I think that there is more value in genuine human feeling than in status and so on. I am just a simple human being. Through my experience and mental discipline, a certain new attitude has developed. This is nothing special. You, who I think have had a better education and more experience than myself, have more potential to change within yourself. I come from a small village with no modern education and no deep awareness of the world. Also, from the age of 15 or 16 I had an unthinkable sort of burden.

~

~

Each of you should feel that you have great potential and that, with self-confidence and a little more effort, change really is possible if you want it. If you feel that your present way of life is unpleasant or has some difficulties, then don't look at these negative things. See the positive side, the potential, and make an effort.

~

~

So, as far as our contact with fellow human beings is concerned, our mental attitude is very crucial. Even for a non-believer, just a simple honest being, the ultimate source of happiness is in our mental attitude. Even if you have good health, material facilities used in the proper way and good relations with other human beings, the main cause of a happy life is within.

~

~

Now you can see how to minimize anger and hatred. First, it is extremely important to realize the negativeness of these emotions in general, particularly hatred. I consider hatred to be the ultimate enemy. By 'enemy' I mean the person or factor which directly or indirectly destroys our interest. Our interest is that which ultimately creates happiness.

~

~

We can also speak of the external enemy. For example, in my own case, our Chinese brothers and sisters are destroying Tibetan rights and, in that way, more suffering and anxiety develops. But no matter how forceful this is, it cannot destroy the supreme source of my happiness, which is my calmness of mind. This is something an external enemy cannot destroy. Our country can be invaded, our possessions can be destroyed, our friends can be killed, but these are secondary for our mental happiness. The ultimate source of my mental happiness is my peace of mind. Nothing can destroy this except my own anger.

~

~

Moreover, you can escape or hide from an external enemy and sometimes you can even cheat the enemy. For example, if there is someone who disturbs my peace of my mind, I can escape by locking my door and sitting quietly alone. But I cannot do that with anger! Wherever I go, it is always there. Even though I have locked my room, the anger is still inside. Unless you adopt a certain method, there is no possibility of escape. Therefore, hatred or anger – and here I mean negative anger – is ultimately the real destroyer of my peace of mind and is therefore my true enemy.

~

~

Some people believe that to suppress emotions is not good, that it is much better to let it out. I think there are differences between various negative emotions. For example, with frustration, there is a certain frustration which develops as a result of past events. Sometimes if you hide these negative events, such as sexual abuse, then consciously or unconsciously this creates problems. Therefore, in this case it is much better to express the frustration and let it out.

~

~

However, according to our experience with anger, if you do not make an attempt to reduce it, it will remain with you and even increase. Then even with small incidents you will immediately get angry. Once you try to control or discipline your anger, then eventually even big events will not cause anger.

~

~

When anger comes there is one important technique to help you keep your peace of mind. You should not become dissatisfied or frustrated, because this is the cause of anger and hatred. There is a natural connection between cause and effect. Once certain causes and conditions are fully met it is extremely difficult to prevent that causal process from coming to fruition. It is crucial to examine the situation so that at a very early stage one is able to put a stop to the causal process. Then it does not continue to an advanced stage.

~

~

In the Buddhist text *A Guide to the Bodhisattva Way of Life*, the great scholar Shantideva mentions that it is very important to ensure that a person does not get into a situation which leads to dissatisfaction, because dissatisfaction is the seed of anger. This means that one must adopt a certain outlook towards one's material possessions, towards one's companions and friends, and towards various situations.

~

~

Our feelings of dissatisfaction, unhappiness, loss of hope and so forth are in fact related to all phenomena. If we do not adopt the right outlook, it is possible that anything and everything could cause us frustration. Yet phenomena are part of reality and we are subject to the laws of existence. So this leaves us only one option: to change our own attitude. By bringing about a change in our outlook towards things and events, all phenomena can become friends or sources of happiness, instead of becoming enemies or sources of frustration.

~

~

In one way, having an enemy is very bad. It disturbs our mental peace and destroys some of our good things. But if we look at it from another angle, only an enemy gives us the opportunity to practise patience. No one else provides us with the opportunity for tolerance. Since we do not know the majority of the five billion human beings on this earth, therefore the majority of people do not give us an opportunity to show tolerance or patience either. Only those people whom we know and who create problems for us really provide us with a good opportunity to practise tolerance and patience.

~

~

Shantideva says that it is the very intention of harming us which makes the enemy very special. If the enemy had no intention of harming us, then we would not classify that person as an enemy, therefore our attitude would be completely different. It is his or her very intention of harming us which makes that person an enemy and because of that the enemy provides us with an opportunity to practise tolerance and patience. Therefore an enemy is indeed a precious teacher. By thinking along these lines you can eventually reduce the negative mental emotions, particularly hatred.

~

~

Another question is that if you always remain humble then others may take advantage of you and how should you react? It is quite simple: you should act with wisdom or common sense, without anger and hatred. If the situation is such that you need some sort of action on your part, you can, without anger, take a counter-measure. In fact, such actions which follow true wisdom rather than anger are in reality more effective. A counter-measure taken in the midst of anger may often go wrong. Without anger and without hatred, we can manage more effectively.

~

~

There is another type of practice of tolerance which involves consciously taking on the sufferings of others. I am thinking of situations in which, by engaging in certain activities, we are aware of the hardships, difficulties and problems that are involved in the short term, but are convinced that such actions will have a very beneficial long-term effect. Because of our attitude and our commitment and wish to bring about that long-term benefit, we sometimes consciously and deliberately take upon ourselves the hardships and problems that are involved in the short term.

~

~

I am quite sure that if this Fourteenth Dalai Lama smiled less, perhaps I would have fewer friends in various places. My attitude towards other people is to always look at them from the human level. On that level, whether president, queen or beggar, there is no difference, provided that there is genuine human feeling with a genuine human smile of affection.

~

PART FOUR

GIVING AND
RECEIVING

~

Compassion is the most wonderful and precious thing. When we talk about compassion, it is encouraging to note that basic human nature is, I believe, compassionate and gentle. For example, one scientist has told me that the first few weeks after birth is the most important period, for during that time the child's brain is enlarging. During that period, the mother's touch or that of someone who is acting like a mother is crucial. This shows that even though the child may not realize who is who, it somehow physically needs someone else's affection. Without that, it is very damaging for the healthy development of the brain.

~

~

When we go to a hospital, irrespective of the doctor's quality, if the doctor shows genuine feeling and deep concern for us, and if he or she smiles, then we feel OK. But if the doctor shows little human affection, then even though he or she may be a very great expert, we may feel unsure and nervous. This is human nature.

~

~

In education, it is my experience that those lessons which we learn from teachers who are not just good, but who also show affection for the student, go deep into our minds. Lessons from other sorts of teachers may not. Although you may be compelled to study and may fear the teacher, the lessons may not sink in. Much depends on the affection from the teacher.

~

~

When we are young and again when we are old, we depend heavily on the affection of others. Between these stages we usually feel that we can do everything without help from others and that other people's affection is simply not important. But at this stage I think it is very important to keep deep human affection.

~

~

When people in a big town or city feel lonely, this does not mean that they lack human companions, but rather that they lack human affection. As a result of this, their mental health eventually becomes very poor. On the other hand, those people who grow up in an atmosphere of human affection have a much more positive and gentle development of their bodies, their minds and their behaviour.

~

~

Children who have grown up lacking a positive atmosphere usually have more negative attitudes. This very clearly shows the basic human nature. Also, as I have mentioned, the human body appreciates peace of mind. Things that are disturbing to us have a very bad effect upon our health. This shows that the whole structure of our health is such that it is suited to an atmosphere of human affection. Therefore, our potential for compassion is there. The only issue is whether or not we realize this and utilize it.

~

~

The basic aim of my explanation is to show that by nature we are compassionate, that compassion is something very necessary and something which we can develop. It is important to know the exact meaning of compassion. The Buddhist interpretation is that genuine compassion is based on a clear acceptance or recognition that others, like oneself, want happiness and have the right to overcome suffering. On that basis one develops some kind of concern about the welfare of others, irrespective of their attitude to oneself. That is compassion.

~

~

Your love and compassion towards your friends is in many cases actually attachment. This feeling is not based on the realization that all beings have an equal right to be happy and to overcome suffering. Instead, it is based on the idea that something is 'mine', 'my friend' or something good for 'me'. That is attachment. Thus, when the person's attitude towards you changes, your feeling of closeness immediately disappears. With the other way, you develop some kind of concern irrespective, of the other person's attitude to you, simply because that person is a fellow human being and has every right to overcome suffering. Whether that person remains neutral to you or even becomes your enemy, your concern should remain.

~

Actually genuine compassion and attachment are contradictory. According to Buddhist practice, to develop genuine compassion you must first practise the meditation of equalization and equanimity, detaching oneself from those people who are very close to you. Then, you must remove negative feelings towards your enemies. All sentient beings should be looked on as equal. On that basis, you can gradually develop genuine compassion for all of them.

~

~

It must be said that genuine compassion is not like pity or a feeling that others are somehow lower than you. Rather, with genuine compassion you view others as more important than yourself.

~

~

In order to generate genuine compassion, first of all one must go through the training of equanimity. This becomes very important because without a sense of equanimity towards all, one's feelings towards others will be biased. So now I will give you a brief example of a Buddhist meditative training on developing equanimity. You should think about, first, a small group of people whom you know, such as your friends and relatives, towards whom you have attachment. Second, you should think about some people to whom you feel totally indifferent. And third, think about some people whom you dislike.

~

~

Once you have imagined these different people, you should try to let your mind go into its natural state and see how it would normally respond to an encounter with these people. You will notice that your natural reaction would be that of attachment towards your friends, that of dislike towards the people whom you consider your enemies and that of total indifference towards those whom you consider neutral. Then you should try to question yourself.

~

~

You should compare the effects of the two opposing attitudes you have towards your friends and your en-emies, and see why you should have such fluctuating states of mind towards these two different groups of people. You should see what effects such reactions have on your mind and try to see the futility of relating to them in such an extreme manner.

~

~

I have already discussed the pros and cons of harbouring hatred and generating anger towards enemies, and I have also spoken a little about the defects of being extremely attached towards friends and so on. You should reflect upon this and then try to minimize your strong emotions towards these two opposing groups of people. Then most importantly, you should reflect on the fundamental equality between yourself and all other sentient beings.

~

~

Just as you have the instinctive natural desire to
be happy and overcome suffering, so do all sentient beings; just as you have the right to fulful
this innate aspiration, so do all sentient beings. So
on what exact grounds do you discriminate?

~

~

If we look at humanity as a whole, we are social animals. Moreover, the structures of the modern economy, education and so on, illustrate that the world has become a smaller place and that we heavily depend on one another. Under such circumstances, I think the only option is to live and work together harmoniously and keep in our minds the interest of the whole of humanity. That is the only outlook and way we must adopt for our survival.

~

~

By nature, especially as a human being, my interests are not independent of others. My happiness depends on others' happiness. So when I see happy people, automatically I also feel a little bit happier than when I see people in a difficult situation. For example, when we see pictures on television which show people starving in Somalia, including old people and young children then we automatically feel sad, regardless of whether that sadness can lead to some kind of active help or not.

~

~

In our daily lives we are now utilizing many good facilities, including things like air-conditioned houses. All these things or facilities became possible, not because of ourselves, but because of many other people's direct or indirect involvement. Everything comes together. It is impossible to return to the way of life of a few centuries ago, when we depended on simple instruments, not all these machines. It is very clear to us that the facilities that we are enjoying now are the products of the activities of many people.

~

~

Since we all have an equal right to be happy and since we are all linked to one another, no matter how important an individual is, logically the interest of the other five billion people on the planet is more important than that of one single person. By thinking along these lines, you can eventually develop a sense of global respon-sibility. Modern environmental problems, such as depletion of the ozone layer, also clearly show us the need for world co-operation. It seems that with development, the whole world has become much smaller, but the human consciousness is still lagging behind.

~

~

A wider or more altruistic attitude is very relevant in today's world. If we look at the situation from various angles, such as the complexity and inter-connectedness of the nature of modern existence, then we will gradually notice a change in our outlook, so that when we say 'others' and when we think of others, we will no longer dismiss them as something that is irrelevant to us. We will no longer feel indifferent.

~

If you think only of yourself, if you forget the rights and well-being of others, or, worse still, if you exploit others, ultimately you will lose. You will have no friends who will show concern for your well-being. Moreover, if a tragedy befalls you, instead of feeling concerned, others might even secretly rejoice. By contrast, if an individual is compassionate and altruistic, and has the interests of others in mind, then irrespective of whether that person knows a lot of people, wherever that person moves, he or she will immediately make friends. And when that person faces a tragedy, there will be plenty of people who will come to help.

~

A true friendship develops on the basis of human affection, not money or power. Of course, due to your power or wealth, more people may approach you with big smiles or gifts. But deep down these are not real friends of yours; these are friends of your wealth or power. As long as your fortune remains, then these people will often approach you. But when your fortunes decline, they will no longer be there. With this type of friend, nobody will make a sincere effort to help you if you need it. That is the reality.

~

~

Genuine human friendship is on the basis of human affection, irrespective of your position. Therefore, the more you show concern about the welfare and rights of others, the more you are a genuine friend. The more you remain open and sincere, then ultimately more benefits will come to you. If you forget or do not bother about others, then eventually you will lose your own benefit.

~

~

There are various positive side effects of enhancing one's feeling of compassion. One of them is that the greater the force of your compassion, the greater your resilience in confronting hardships and your ability to transform them into more positive conditions.

~

~

One form of practice that seems to be quite effective in enhancing compassion is found in *A Guide to the Bodhisattva Way of Life*, a classic Buddhist text. In this practice you visualize your old self, the embodiment of self-centredness, selfishness and so on, and then visualize a group of people who represent the masses of other sentient beings. Then you adopt a third per-son's point of view as a neutral, unbiased observer and make a comparative assessment of the value, the interests and then the importance of these two groups. You will naturally begin to feel more inclined towards the countless others.

~

~

I also think that the greater the force of your altruistic attitude towards sentient beings, the more courageous you become. The greater your courage, the less you feel prone to discouragement and loss of hope. Therefore, compassion is also a source of inner strength.

~

~

With increased inner strength it is possible to develop firm determination and with determination there is a greater chance of success, no matter what obstacles there may be. On the other hand, if you feel hesitation, fear and lack of self-confidence, then often you will develop a pessimistic attitude. I consider that to be the real seed of failure. Therefore, even in the conventional sense, compassion is very important for a successful future.

~

~

Having reflected upon the faults of a self-centred way of thinking and life, and also having reflected upon the positive consequences of being mindful of the well-being of other sentient beings and working for their benefit, and being convinced of this, then in Buddhist meditation there is a special training which is known as 'the practice of Giving and Taking'. Using visualization, it basically involves taking upon yourself all the suffering pain, negativity and undesirable experiences of other sentient beings.

~

~

You imagine taking this suffering upon yourself and then giving away or sharing with others your own positive qualities, such as your virtuous states of mind, your positive energy, your wealth, your happiness and so forth. Such a form of training, psychologically brings about a transformation in your mind so effectively that your feeling of love and compassion is much more enhanced.

~

~

One thing you should remember is that mental transformations take time and are not easy. I think some people from the West, where technology is so good, think that everything is automatic. You should not expect this spiritual transformation to take place within a short period; that is impossible. Keep it in your mind and make a constant effort, then after 1 year, 5 years, 10 years, 15 years, you will eventually find some change. I still sometimes find it very difficult to practice these things. However, I really do believe that these practices are extremely useful.

~

~

My favourite quotation from Shantideva's book is: 'As long as space endures, as long as sentient beings remain, until then, may I too remain and dispel the miseries of the world.'

~

PART FIVE

TRANSFORMING
THE MIND

The Eight Verses on Transforming the Mind is one of the most important texts from a genre of Tibetan spiritual writings known as the *lo-jong*, literally 'transforming the mind.' Written by the eleventh-century Tibetan master Langri Thangpa, this short work is one of His Holiness the Dalai Lama's main sources of inspiration.

Central themes of the *lo-jong* teachings include, amongst others, the enhancement of compassion, the cultivation of balanced attitudes toward self and others, the development of positive ways of thinking, and the transformation of adverse situations into conditions favorable to spiritual development.

The whole point of transforming our heart and mind is to find happiness. We all have the natural desire to be happy and the wish to overcome suffering. This is a fact, so we can make it our starting-point.

Before developing this point in more detail, however, let us look very briefly at the nature of experience. Broadly speaking, our experiences fall into two categories. One type of experience is more connected with our bodies, and occurs mainly through our sense organs, while the other type is more related to what can be called 'the mental consciousness' or 'the mind.'

~

So far as the physical level of experience is concerned, there is not much difference between ourselves and other animal species. Animals, too, have the capacity to feel both pain and well-being. But what perhaps distinguishes us human beings from other forms of life is that we have far more powerful mental experiences in the form of thoughts and emotions.

~

~

The fact that there are two broad categories of experience has some interesting implications. Most importantly, if a person's basic state of mind is serene and calm, then it is possible for this inner peace to overwhelm a painful physical experience. On the other hand, if someone is suffering from depression, anxiety, or any form of emotional distress, then even if he or she happens to be enjoying physical comforts, he will not really be able to experience the happiness that these could bring. So this shows that our state of mind, in terms of our attitudes and emotions, plays a crucial role in shaping the way we experience happiness and suffering. The *lo-jong* teachings on

~

transforming the mind offer a series of methods by which we can channel and discipline our mind, and so create the basis for the happiness we are seeking.

~

~

We all know that there is an intimate connection between physical well-being and emotional well-being. We know, for example, that physical illnesses affect our state of mind, and that, conversely, a greater degree of physical well-being contributes towards greater mental ease. Since we commonly recognize this correlation, many of us engage in physical practices and exercises to help bring about that physical well-being which will contribute to our mental refreshment. There are also certain traditional practices that are aimed at training our energy patterns; these are called *prana yogas*, or 'yogas of the wind energy.' These days, yogic exercises have become very popular in the

~

modern world, too, and this is precisely because many people have found that through yoga they can achieve a degree of physical health that leads to better mental health. The approach that is suggested by the *lo-jong* teachings is slightly different, however. They concentrate directly on the development of the mind itself, through the transformation of our attitudes and ways of thinking.

~

~

The key to transforming our hearts and minds is to have an understanding of the way our thoughts and emotions work. We need to learn how to identify the opposing sides in our inner conflicts. With anger, for example, we need to see how destructive anger is, and, at the same time, realize that there are antidotes within our own thoughts and emotions that we can use to counter it. So, first, by understanding that afflictive thoughts and emotions are destructive and negative, and, second, by trying to strengthen our positive thoughts and emotions, which are their antidotes, we can gradually reduce the force of our anger, hatred and so on.

~

~

The way to examine how thoughts and emotions arise in us is through introspection. It is quite natural for many different thoughts and emotions to arise. When we leave them unexamined and untamed this leads to untold problems, crises, suffering and misery. This is why we need to adopt the conscious discipline we spoke of earlier: in order to reduce the power of a negative emotion like anger or hatred, we need to encourage its antidote, which is love and compassion.

~

It is not enough to recognize that this is what is required, just as it is not enough simply to wish that love and compassion should increase in us. We have to make a sustained effort, again and again, to cultivate the positive aspects within us, and the key here is constant familiarity. The nature of human thoughts and emotions is such that the more you engage in them, and the more you develop them, the more powerful they become. Therefore we have to develop love and compassion consciously in order to enhance their strength. We are, in fact, talking about a way of cultivating habits that are positive. We do this through meditation.

~

MEDITATION:
A SPIRITUAL DISCIPLINE

What do we understand by meditation? From the Buddhist point of view, meditation is a spiritual discipline, and one that allows you to have some degree of control over your thoughts and emotions.

Why is it that we don't succeed in enjoying the lasting happiness that we are seeking? Buddhism explains that our normal state of mind is such that our thoughts and emotions are wild and unruly, and since we lack the mental discipline needed to tame them, we are powerless to control them. As a result, they control us. And thoughts and

~

emotions, in their turn, tend to be controlled by
our negative impulses rather than our positive
ones. We need to reverse this cycle.

~

~

The idea of bringing about such a fundamental change in ourselves may at first sight seem impossible, yet it is actually possible to do this through a process of discipline such as meditation. We choose a particular object, and then we train our minds by developing our ability to remain focused on the object. Normally, if we just take a moment to reflect, we will see that our mind is not focused at all. We may be thinking about something and, all of a sudden, we find that we have been distracted because something else came into our head. Our thoughts are constantly chasing after this and that because we don't have the discipline of having a focus. So, through meditation, what we

~

can achieve is the ability to place our minds and to focus our attention at will on any given object.

~

~

Now of course, we could choose to focus on a negative object in our meditation. If, for example, you are infatuated with someone, and if you focus your mind single-pointedly on that person, and then dwell on their desirable qualities, this will have the effect of increasing your sexual desire for that person. But this is not what meditation is for. From a Buddhist point of view, meditation has to be practiced in relation to a positive object, by which we mean an object that will enhance your ability to focus. Through that familiarity you become closer and closer to the object and feel a sense of intimacy with it. In the classical Buddhist literature this type of meditation is described

~

as *shamatha*, tranquil abiding, which is a single-pointed meditation.

~

Shamatha alone is not sufficient. In Buddhism, we combine single-pointed meditation with the practice of analytic meditation, which is known as *vipasyana*, penetrative insight. In this practice we apply reasoning. By recognizing the strengths and weaknesses of different types of emotions and thoughts, together with their advantages and disadvantages, we are able to enhance our positive states of mind which contribute towards a sense of serenity, tranquility, and contentment, and to reduce those attitudes and emotions that lead to suffering and dissatisfaction. Reasoning thus plays a helpful part in this process.

~

Whatever forms of meditation you practice, the most important point is to apply mindfulness continuously, and make a sustained effort. It is unrealistic to expect results from meditation within a short period of time. What is required is continuous sustained effort.

~

PART SIX

TRANSFORMING
THROUGH ALTRUISM

~

THE QUALITIES OF
BODHICHITTA, THE ALTRUISTIC
INTENTION

The definition of bodhichitta is given in Maitreya's *Ornament of Realization*, where he states that there are two aspects to altruism. The first is the condition that produces the altruistic outlook, and this involves the compassion that a person must develop towards all sentient beings, and the aspiration he or she must cultivate to bring about the welfare of all sentient beings. This leads to the second aspect, which is the wish to attain

~

enlightenment. It is for the sake of benefitting all beings that this wish should arise in us.

~

~

We could say that bodhichitta is the highest level of altruism and the highest form of courage, and we could also say that bodhichitta is the outcome of the highest altruistic activity. As Lama Tsongkhapa explains in his *Great Exposition of the Path to Enlightenment*, bodhichitta is such that while one engages in fulfilling the wishes of others, the fulfillment of one's own self-interest comes as a by-product. This is a wise way of benefitting both oneself and others. In fact I think bodhichitta is really and truly wonderful. The more I think of helping others, and the stronger my feeling for taking care of others becomes, the more benefit I reap myself. That is quite extraordinary.

~

In a sense we could say that the practice of generating and cultivating the altruistic intention is so comprehensive that it contains the essential elements of all other spiritual practices. Taken alone, it can therefore replace the practice of many different techniques, since all other methods are distilled into one approach. This is why we consider that bodhichitta practice lies at the root of both temporary and lasting happiness. Now the question is how we can train ourselves to develop bodhichitta. The two aspects of bodhichitta that we spoke about earlier, the aspiration to be of help to others and the aspiration to attain enlightenment oneself, have to be cultivated separately

~

through separate trainings. The aspiration to be of
help to others has to be cultivated first.

~

~

The Two Altruistic Aspirations

1. The aspiration to attain enlightenment

The highest form of spiritual practice is the cultivation of the altruistic intention to attain enlightenment for the benefit of all sentient beings, known as bodhichitta. This is the most precious state of mind, the supreme source of benefit and goodness, that which fulfills both our immediate and ultimate aspirations, and the basis of altruistic activity. However, bodhichitta can only be realized through regular concerted effort, so in order to attain it we need to cultivate the

~

discipline necessary for training and transforming
our mind.

~

~

As we discussed earlier, the transformation of mind and heart does not happen overnight but through a gradual process. Although it is true that in some cases instantaneous spiritual experiences may be possible, they are rather unreliable and somewhat shortlived. The problem is that when sudden experiences occur, like bolts of lightning, the individual may feel profoundly moved and inspired, but if the experiences are not grounded in discipline and sustained effort they are very unpredictable, and their transformative impact will be rather limited. By contrast, a genuine transformation that results from sustained concerted effort is long-lasting because it has a firm foundation. This is why

~

long-term spiritual transformation can really only
come about through a gradual process of training
and discipline.

~

~

The potential for perfection, the potential for full enlightenment, actually lies within each one of us. In fact this potential is nothing other than the essential nature of the mind itself, which is said to be the mere nature of luminosity and knowing. Through the gradual process of spiritual practice, we can eliminate the obstructions that hinder us from perfecting this seed of enlightenment. As we overcome them, step by step, so the inherent quality of our consciousness begins to become more and more manifest until it reaches the highest stage of perfection, which is none other than the enlightened mind of the Buddha.

~

2. Working for the welfare of others

The other aspiration of the altruistic intention (bodhichitta) is the wish to bring about the welfare of other sentient beings. Welfare, in the Buddhist sense, means helping others to attain total freedom from suffering, and the term 'other sentient beings' refers to the infinite number of beings in the universe. This aspiration is really the key to the first, namely the intention to attain enlightenment for the benefit of all sentient beings. It is founded on genuine compassion towards all sentient beings equally. Compassion here means the wish that all other beings should be free of suffering. So it is said to be at the root

~

of all altruistic activity and of the altruistic intention as a whole.

~

~

We need to cultivate a compassion that is powerful enough to make us feel committed to bringing about the well-being of others, so that we are actually willing to shoulder the responsibility for making this happen. In Buddhism, such compassion is called 'great compassion.' The point is emphasized again and again that great compassion is the foundation of all positive qualities, the root of the entire Mahayana path, and the heart of bodhichitta. Likewise, Chandrakirti says in his *Entry to the Middle Way* that compassion is such a supreme spiritual quality that it maintains its relevance at all times: it is vital at the initial stage of the spiritual path, it is just as important while

~

we are on the path, and it is equally relevant when an individual has become fully enlightened.

~

~

Generally speaking, as I said, compassion is the wish that others should be free of suffering, but if we look into it more closely compassion has two levels. In one case it may exist simply at the level of a wish – just wishing the other to be free of suffering – but it can also exist on a higher level, where the emotion goes beyond a mere wish to include the added dimension of actually wanting to do something about the suffering of others. In this case, a sense of responsibility and personal commitment enters into the thought and emotion of altruism.

~

~

Whichever level of compassion we may have, for the development of bodhichitta to be successful it must be combined with the complementary factor of wisdom and insight. If you lack wisdom and insight, when you are confronted with another's suffering, genuine compassion may arise in you spontaneously, but given that your resources are limited, you may only be able to make a wish: 'May he or she be free of that pain or suffering.' However, over time that kind of feeling may lead to a feeling of helplessness because you realize you cannot really do anything to change the situation. On the other hand, if you are equipped with wisdom and insight then you have a much greater

~

resource to draw on, and the more you focus on the object of compassion, the greater the intensity of your compassion will be and the more it will increase.

~

~

Because of the way insight and wisdom affect the development of compassion, the Buddhist literature identifies three different types of compassion. First, at the initial stage, compassion is simply the wish to see other sentient beings freed from suffering; it is not reinforced by any particular insight into the nature of suffering or the nature of a sentient being. Then, at the second stage, compassion is not simply the wish to see another being free from suffering, it is strengthened by insight into the transient nature of existence, such as the realization that the being who is the object of your compassion does not exist permanently. When insight complements your compassion it gives it

~

greater power. Finally, at the third stage, compassion is described as 'non-objectifying compassion.' It can be directed towards that same suffering being, but now it is reinforced by a full awareness of the ultimate nature of that being. This is a very powerful type of compassion, because it enables you to engage with the other person without objectifying him or her, and without clinging on to the idea that he or she has any absolute reality.

~

~

Since compassion is the wish that others should be free of suffering, it requires above all the ability to feel connected to other beings. We know from experience that the closer we feel towards a particular person or animal, the greater our capacity to empathize with that being. It follows, then, that an important element in the spiritual practice of developing compassion is the ability to feel empathetic and connected, and to have a sense of closeness with others. Buddhism describes this as a sense of intimacy with the object of compassion; it is also called loving-kindness. The closer you feel towards another being, the more powerfully you will feel that the sight of his or her suffering is unbearable.

~

There are two main methods in Buddhism for cultivating this sense of closeness or intimacy. One is the method known as 'exchanging and equalizing oneself with others.' Although it stems from Nagarjuna, it was more fully developed by Shantideva in his *Guide to the Bodhisattva's Way of Life* (Bodhicaryavatara). The other technique is known as the 'seven-point cause and effect method.' This emphasizes the cultivation of an attitude that enables us to relate to all other beings as we would to someone very dear. The traditional example given is that we should consider all sentient beings as our mother, but some scriptures also include considering beings as our father, or as

~

dear friends, or as close relatives, and so on. Our
mother is simply taken as an example, but the
point is that we should learn to view all other sentient beings as very dear and close to our hearts.

~

It seems that for some the seven-point cause and effect method is more effective, while for others the technique of exchanging and equalizing self with others appears to be more effective, depending upon the individual's inclinations and mentality. However, within the Tibetan tradition the custom really has been to combine both these methods so that one can enjoy the benefits of practicing both approaches.

THE SEVEN-POINT CAUSE AND
EFFECT METHOD

The seven points are: recognizing that all sentient beings have been our mother in a past life; reflecting on the kindness of all beings; meditating on repaying their kindness; meditating on love; meditating on compassion; generating the extraordinary attitude of universal responsibility; and the actual development of bodhichitta.

Before we can apply the seven-point cause and effect method to ourselves, we need to cultivate a sense of equanimity towards all sentient beings, which is expressed through the ability to relate to

~

all others equally. To do this, we need to address the problem of having thoughts and emotions that fluctuate. Not only should we try to overcome extreme negative emotions like anger and hatred, but also, in this particular spiritual practice, we should try to work with the attachment we feel to our loved ones.

~

~

Now, of course, in this attachment to loved ones there is a sense of closeness and intimacy, as well as an element of love, compassion and affection, but often these emotions are also tinged with a strong feeling of desire. The reason for that is rather obvious, because when we relate to people towards whom we feel deeply attached, our feelings are highly susceptible to emotional extremes. When such a person does something that is contrary to our expectations, for instance, it has a much greater potential to hurt us than if the same thing were done by someone to whom we do not feel that close. This indicates that in the affection we feel there is a high degree of attachment. So, in

~

this particular spiritual practice, we try to level out the attachment we have to certain people, so that our sense of closeness to them is genuine and not tinged with desire.

~

~

The key point in this preliminary practice of equanimity is to overcome the feelings of partiality and discrimination that we normally feel towards others, based on the fluctuating emotions and thoughts associated with closeness and distance. It really seems to be true that attachment constrains our vision, so that we are not able to see things from a wider perspective.

~

~

Recently I was at a seminar on science and religion in Argentina, and one of the participant scientists made a point which I think is very true. He said that it is very important for research scientists to adopt the methodological principle of not being emotionally attached to their field of inquiry. This is because attachment has the negative effect of clouding and narrowing your vision. I totally agree. This is why, through the practice of equanimity, we try to overcome these feelings of partiality so that we can deal with everything and relate to everyone even-handedly.

~

~

When we practice developing equanimity, sometimes it is helpful to use visualization. For example, you can imagine three different individuals in front of you: someone who is very close to you, someone you regard as an enemy and whom you dislike, and then someone who is completely neutral and to whom you feel indifferent. Then let your natural emotions and thoughts arise in relation to these three individuals. Once you are able to allow your natural feelings to arise, you will notice that towards the loved one you feel a sense of closeness and also great attachment, towards the person you dislike you may feel hostility and a sense of distance, and that towards

~

the individual who is neutral you will hardly feel
any emotion at all.

~

~

At this point, try to reason with yourself. 'Why do I feel such different emotions towards these three individuals? Why do I feel so attached to my loved ones?' You might begin to see that there are certain grounds for your attachment: the person is dear to you because he or she has done this and that for you, and so on. But if you then ask yourself whether these characteristics are permanent and whether the person will always be like this, then you may have to concede that this is not necessarily the case. Someone may be a friend today but turn into an enemy tomorrow. This is especially true from the Buddhist point of view, when we take many lifetimes into account –

~

someone who is very close to you in this life may have been your enemy in another. From this perspective there are no real grounds for feeling such strong attachment.

~

~

In the same way, then turn your attention towards the person you dislike and ask yourself, 'On what grounds do I feel such negative emotions towards this person?' Again, this may be because he or she has done certain things towards you. But then ask yourself whether that person is likely to remain your enemy all his life. And then, if you take into account the question of many lifetimes, you will realize that the individual may have been very close to you in a past life, so his status as your enemy is merely short term. You begin to see that there are no justifiable grounds for having such extreme hatred and anger towards that person.

~

~

Finally, consider the individual in the middle, to whom you feel totally indifferent. If you raise the same kind of questions again, you will realize that the person may have very little relevance to your present life but may have been important to you in other lives in the past; and even in this lifetime, he may become important to you at some future point. So this type of visualization helps to level out the extreme fluctuating emotions that you feel towards others, and to establish a stable basis on which you can build a more balanced sense of closeness. If we think along these lines, and question our emotions from various angles, then we come to appreciate that the extreme emotions that

~

we tend to feel towards others, and the behaviors they generate, are perhaps unwise.

~

~

Thinking of Others as Someone Dear

Having developed equanimity, we can begin the first stage of the seven-point practice, which is cultivating the attitude of thinking of all others as being as dear to you as your mother, or father, or friend. Here, of course, the teachings take into account the idea of beginningless lifetimes, so all other sentient beings are considered to have been our mother or father or friend at one point or another. This is the way we try to relate to others and to develop a genuine sense of connection.

~

~

The reason this practice is traditionally considered so important is because, in nature, it is predominantly mothers who play the most critical role in nurturing and bringing up their offspring. In some animal species both mother and father remain together to look after their young, but in most cases it is just the mother. There are some exceptions, of course. There are some species of bird where the mother hardly participates at all in the building of the nest; it is the male that works hard to build the nest while the female just looks on and inspects the result! It then seems quite fair that the male takes greater responsibility in the nurturing process. However, such cases are rare.

It is for these reasons that traditional Indian and Tibetan texts single out mothers as an example of how we should relate to other beings. In fact the Tibetan language has coined a special term for 'dear old mother sentient beings,' and the expression has become so deeply embedded in people's psyche, it has a poetic ring to it. Nowadays, whenever people raise gender issues in the context of Tibetan culture, I tell them that for me the whole idea of 'mother sentient beings,' and the Tibetan expression that goes with it, is a good example of how motherhood was valued in Buddhist culture.

~

In the traditional literature, it is understood that this profound recognition of all sentient beings as being like one's mother is based upon the notion of successive lifetimes, so the whole question of rebirth and past lives comes into the picture here. The Buddhist teachings emphasize the need to understand the possibility of rebirth on the basis of understanding the nature of consciousness. The point is made that consciousness is a phenomenon that arises due only to a previous moment of consciousness. Matter cannot become consciousness. As regards the connection between mind and matter generally, one can contribute towards the causation of the other, but in terms of an

~

individual continuum, consciousness must be caused by a preceding moment of consciousness.

~

~

Reflecting on the Kindness of All Beings

The second element of the seven-point cause and effect method is reflecting upon the kindness of all beings. In your meditation, you focus on the kindness of others, especially in the context that they have been your mother in this or other lifetimes, and this naturally leads to the thought, 'I must repay their kindness. I must acknowledge the profound kindness they have shown to me.' Such feelings will arise naturally in someone who is honorable, ethical, and what we could call 'civilized.'

~

~

Once you recognize all other beings as your kind, dear mothers then naturally you will feel close to them. With this as a basis, you should cultivate love or loving-kindness, which is traditionally defined as the wish to see others enjoy happiness, and then you also develop compassion, which is the wish for others to be free of suffering. Love and compassion are two sides of the same coin.

~

~

Exchanging and Equalizing Oneself with Others

We will now turn to the other method for transforming the mind, which is exchanging and equalizing oneself with others. Here again, the first stage is the cultivation of equanimity, although the meaning of equanimity in this context is different from the one we spoke of earlier. Here, equanimity is understood as the fundamental equality of all beings, in the sense that just as you have the spontaneous wish to be happy and overcome suffering, so does every single other being, in equal measure.

~

~

Now we try to probe deeper to understand what this aspiration to be free of suffering really implies. It does not arise from a sense of self-importance, or self-congratulation; such considerations simply do not play any role here at all. This basic aspiration arises in us simply by virtue of the fact that we are conscious living beings. Together with this aspiration comes a conviction that I, as an individual, have a legitimate right to fulfill my aspiration. If we accept this, then we can relate the same principle to others and we will realize that everyone else shares this basic aspiration too. Therefore, if I as an individual have the right to fulfill my aspiration, then others, too, have an equal right to fulfill theirs. It is on these grounds that one has to recognize the fundamental equality of all beings.

~

Within the practice of equalizing and exchanging oneself with others, this is the equalizing stage, where we develop the understanding that we and others are fundamentally equal. The next stage involves reflecting on the shortcomings of excessively self-cherishing thoughts, and their negative consequences, as well as reflecting on the merits of developing thoughts that cherish the well-being of others.

~

~

How do we do this? We begin by comparing ourselves with others. We have accepted that there is a fundamental equality between ourselves and others in terms of our respective aspirations to be happy and overcome suffering, and we have also recognized that all beings, including ourselves, have an equal right to fulfill that aspiration. No matter how important an individual person may be, and no matter how unimportant, in a worldly sense, others may be, so far as the basic fact of wishing to be happy and overcome suffering is concerned, there is absolute equality. So what is the difference between us? The difference is really a matter of numbers. No matter how important

~

an individual is, the interest of that individual is
the interest of only one being, whereas the interest
of others is the interest of an infinite number
of beings.

~

The question is, which is more important? Simply from the numerical point of view, if we want to be fair we have to accept that the interest of others is more important than our own. Even in the mundane world we know that the issues which affect the lives of many people are generally granted greater significance than those that affect fewer people or a single individual. So, logically, one has to accept that the well-being of others is more important than one's own. To be completely rational or objective, one could say that sacrificing the interest of the many for the sake of one person is an unwise and foolish act, whereas sacrificing the interest of one individual for the benefit of an

~

infinite number of others is more rational, if such
a choice is necessary.

~

~

Now, you might think that all of this sounds fine, but at the end of the day you are 'you' and others are 'other.' If self and others are totally independent of each other, and there is no connection whatsoever between them, then perhaps there is a case for ignoring the well-being of others and simply pursuing one's own self-interest. However, this is not the case. Self and others are not really independent; in fact, their respective interests are intertwined.

~

~

From the Buddhist point of view, even when you are unenlightened your life is so intertwined with those of others that you cannot really carve yourself out as a single isolated individual. Also, when you follow a spiritual path, many spiritual realizations depend on your interaction with others, so here again others are indispensable. Even when you have attained the highest state of enlightenment, your enlightened activities are for the benefit of others. Indeed, enlightened activity comes about spontaneously by virtue of the fact that other beings exist, so others are indispensable even at that stage. Your life and the lives of others are so interconnected that the idea of a self that is

~

totally distinct and independent of others really does not make any sense.

~

Although this is the reality, it is not reflected in our
behavior. Until now, regardless of reality, we have
nurtured within ourselves a whole complex of self-
cherishing thoughts. We believe in something that
we hold very dear and we regard as precious,
something that is like the core of our being; and
this is accompanied by a powerful belief in our
existence as an individual being with an independent reality. The belief that there is a substantially
real self, and the cherishing of one's own interest
at the expense of others, are the two main
thoughts and emotions we have nurtured within
us throughout our many lives. But what is the
result of this? What benefit does it bring? We are

~

continually suffering, we are continually experiencing negative thoughts and emotions, so our self-cherishing hasn't really got us very far.

~

~

If we shift our focus from ourselves to others and
to the wider world, and if we turn our attention to
all the crises in the world, all the difficulties and
the sufferings and so on, we will see that many of
these problems are direct or indirect consequences
of undisciplined negative states of mind. And
where do these come from? From this powerful
combination of self-centeredness and the belief in
our independent existence. By shifting our attention to the wider world in this way, we can begin
to appreciate the immensely destructive consequences of such thinking.

~

~

These attitudes are not helpful even from one's own selfish point of view. We might ask ourselves, 'What benefit do I as an individual derive from my self-centeredness, and from the belief in my existence as an independent self?' When you really think deeply, you will realize the answer is 'Not very much.'

~

~

In fact, these beliefs are the source of suffering and misery even for the individual. The Buddhist literature is full of discussions on this. Interestingly, about two years ago, I was at a medical conference in America, and a participating psychologist presented the findings of research he had carried out over a long period of time. One conclusion he considered almost indisputable was that there seems to be a correlation between early death, high blood pressure and heart disease on one side, and a disproportionately high use of first personal pronouns on the other ('I', 'me,' and 'mine'). I thought this finding was very interesting. Even scientific studies seem to suggest that there is a

~

correlation between excessive self-cherishing and damage to one's physical well-being.

~

~

Now in contrast, if you shift your focus from yourself to others, extend your concern to others, and cultivate the thought of caring for the well-being of others, then this will have the immediate effect of opening up your life and helping you to reach out. In other words, the practice of cultivating altruism has a beneficial effect not only from the religious point of view but also from the mundane point of view, not only for long-term spiritual development but even in terms of immediate rewards. From my own personal experience I can tell you that when I practice altruism and care for others, it immediately makes me calmer and more secure. So altruism brings immediate benefits.

~

The same applies when you cultivate the understanding that the self is not really an independently existing entity, and begin to view self instead in terms of its dependent relation to others. Although it is difficult to say that merely reflecting on this will produce a profound spiritual realization, it will at least have some effect. Your mind will be more open. Something will begin to change within you. Therefore, even in the immediate term there is definitely a positive and beneficial effect in reversing these two attitudes and moving from self-centeredness to other-centeredness, from belief in self-existence to belief in dependent origination.

~

~

To summarize, I agree with Shantideva when he
writes:

What need is there to say more?
The childish work for their own benefit,
The buddhas work for the benefit of others.
Just look at the difference between them.

If I do not exchange my happiness
For the suffering of others,
I shall not attain the state of buddhahood
And even in samsara I shall have no real joy.

~

The source of all misery in the world

Lies in thinking of oneself;

The source of all happiness

Lies in thinking of others.

~

PART SEVEN

TRANSFORMATION
THROUGH INSIGHT

~

INSIGHT INTO THE NATURE
OF SUFFERING

Along with the methods for cultivating a sense of closeness to others there is another key element for developing compassion, and that is deepening our insight into the nature of suffering. The Tibetan tradition maintains that contemplation on suffering is much more effective when it is done on the basis of one's own personal experience, and when it is focused on oneself, because, generally, we tend to be better able to relate to our own suffering than to that of others. This is why two of the principal elements of the Buddhist path, compassion

~

and renunciation, are seen as two sides of the same coin. True renunciation arises when one has a genuine insight into the nature of suffering, focused upon oneself, and true compassion arises when that focus shifts to others; so the difference lies simply in the object of focus.

~

~

So far as the first level of suffering is concerned –
physical pain and other obvious sufferings – we
consider that even animals have the capacity to recognize these experiences as suffering, and they are
also capable of finding relief from some aspect of
them, however temporary that may be. As for the
suffering of change, which is the second category,
this actually refers to experiences that we conventionally identify as pleasurable or happy. These are
subject to the suffering of change, because the more
you indulge in them, the more they lead to dissatisfaction. If these experiences were bringing some
genuine lasting happiness, then the more you
indulged in them the longer the experience of

~

happiness would last, yet that is not the case. All too often what may seem like a pleasurable experience, and what may initially seem like happiness, when pursued, changes at a certain point into suffering and leads to frustration and so on. So even though conventionally it is called happiness, in another sense it has the nature of suffering. In fact, if you examine the nature of pleasurable sensations you will see that there is often an extremely relative dimension to them; we usually define an experience as pleasurable by comparison to a more intense form of suffering that has just come to an end. What we call 'pleasure' or 'happiness' is more like the temporary absence of intense suffering and pain.

~

However, this is not the deeper meaning of suffering that we speak about in Buddhism. The suffering of change is identified as a type of suffering by many other spiritual traditions, too, and there are methods that are common to both Buddhist and non-Buddhist Indian traditions that allow the individual to recognize these experiences as suffering and to gain temporary freedom from it. These methods include various meditative techniques, the cultivation of absorptive states of mind, contemplations, and so on.

~

~

It is the third level of suffering, called 'the suffering of pervasive conditioning,' that we are concerned with here. The suffering of conditioning is the origin of the other two types of suffering. It is the nature of our very existence, which comes about as a result of karma, delusions, and afflictive emotions. Our very existence as unenlightened beings is said to be fundamentally unsatisfactory, or duhkha, that is, suffering. Through the practice of compassion and renunciation, we need to develop a genuine desire to gain freedom from this third level of suffering, but this desire can only arise if we understand the nature of suffering and its causes.

~

~

When you engage in deep contemplation on the nature of suffering, on the causes of suffering, and on the fact that there exist powerful antidotes to those causes, and when you reflect on the possibility of freedom from suffering and its causes, then you will be able to develop genuine renunciation from the depths of your heart, for you will truly aspire to gain freedom from suffering. At this stage, you will have a sense of being completely exhausted by your experience of unenlightened existence, and by the fact that you are under the domination of negative thoughts and emotions.

~

~

After you establish the aspiration to gain freedom from that kind of existence, you can shift that aspiration to others, and focus on others' experience of suffering, which is the same as your own. If you combine that with the reflections we mentioned earlier – recognizing all sentient beings as dear mothers, reflecting upon their kindness, and realizing the fundamental equality of oneself and others – then there is a real possibility for genuine compassion to arise within you. Only then will you have the genuine aspiration to be of benefit to others.

~

PART EIGHT

EIGHT VERSES
ON TRANSFORMING
THE MIND

~

Until now, we have talked about the basis that makes spiritual transformation possible, and about the need for training the mind. The most essential point is the development of bodhichitta, the altruistic intention to attain enlightenment for the sake of all sentient beings, which arises from training in the two aspirations. As a means to enhance our practice it is advised that we should constantly apply it in our daily life, and to our behavior as a whole – physical, verbal, and mental. Verbal action includes reading texts like The Eight Verses on Transforming the Mind, presented here as an aid to constantly remind you of the importance of undertaking this kind of contemplation.

~

The development of bodhichitta is the core of the Buddha's teaching, and the main path. Once the development of bodhichitta has taken place, the practitioner endeavors to apply the altruistic principle throughout his or her life. This leads to what are known as the 'bodhisattva ideals,' including the 'six perfections' – the perfections of generosity, morality, patience, enthusiasm, meditation or concentration, and wisdom.

~

~

The point I wish to make here is that the practice of compassion is at the heart of the entire path. All other practices are either preliminary to it, or a foundation for it, or they are subsequent applications of this core practice. I would also like to point out that there is a consensus between all Buddhist schools on this, in both Mahayana and non-Mahayana traditions. So compassion lies at the root of all the Buddha's teaching, but it is within the bodhisattva ideal that we find special emphasis on the concerted development of compassion by means of cultivating bodhichitta.

~

~

The Eight Verses On Transforming the Mind

With a determination to achieve the highest aim
For the benefit of all sentient beings,
Which surpasses even the wish-fulfilling gem,
May I hold them dear at all times.

In this verse you are making the aspiration to hold
all other sentient beings as supremely dear to you,
because they are the basis upon which you can
achieve the highest goal, which is the welfare of
sentient beings. This goal surpasses even the
legendary wish-fulfilling jewel, because however

~

precious such a jewel may be, it cannot provide the highest spiritual attainment. There is also a reference here to the kindness of all other beings, and we spoke of the meaning of this earlier. It is due to other sentient beings that you can develop great compassion, the highest spiritual principle, and it is thanks to other sentient beings that you can develop bodhichitta, the altruistic intention. So it is on the basis of your interaction with others that you can attain the highest spiritual realizations. From that point of view, the kindness of others is very profound.

~

When we talk of cultivating the thought of holding others as supremely dear, it is important to
understand that we are not cultivating the kind of
pity that we sometimes feel towards someone who
is less fortunate than ourselves. With pity, there
can be a tendency to look down upon the object of
our compassion, and to feel a sense of superiority.
Holding others dear is in fact the reverse of this.
In this practice, by recognizing the kindness of
others and how indispensable they are for our own
spiritual progress, we appreciate their tremendous
importance and significance, and therefore we
naturally accord them a higher status in our minds.
It is because we think of them in this way that we

~

are able to relate to them as dear, and as worthy of our respect and affection. Because of this, the next verse reads:

~

Whenever I interact with someone,
May I view myself as the lowest amongst all,
And, from the very depths of my heart,
Respectfully hold others as superior.

This verse suggests the kind of attitude that I have just described. The idea of seeing oneself as lower than others should not be misconstrued as a way of neglecting ourselves, ignoring our needs, or feeling that we are a hopeless case. Rather, as I explained earlier, it stems from a courageous state of mind where you are able to relate to others, fully aware of what ability you have to help. So please do not misunderstand this point.

~

What is being suggested here is the need for genuine humility.

~

~

I would like to tell a story to illustrate this. There was a great master about two or three generations ago called Dza Patrul Rinpoche. Not only was he a great master but he had a large following, and he would often give teachings to thousands of students. But he was also a meditator, so occasionally he would disappear to do a retreat somewhere, and his students would have to run around to search for him. During one of these breaks he was on a pilgrimage, and he stayed for a couple of days with a family, like many Tibetan pilgrims did; they would seek shelter with a family on the road and do some chores in return for food. So Dza Patrul Rinpoche did various chores for the family,

~

including emptying the mother's potty, which he
did on a regular basis.

~

Eventually some of his students arrived in that region, and heard that Dza Patrul Rinpoche was somewhere around, and a number of monks finally reached this household and approached the mother of the house. 'Do you know where Dza Patrul Rinpoche is?' they asked. 'I don't know of any Dza Patrul Rinpoche around here,' she replied. The monks then described him to her, and added, 'We heard he was living in your house as a pilgrim.' 'Oh,' she cried, 'that is Dza Patrul Rinpoche!' Apparently, just at that moment, Dza Patrul Rinpoche had gone to empty her potty. The mother was so horrified that she ran away!

~

What this story tells us is that even in a great lama like Dza Patrul Rinpoche, who had a following of thousands, and who was used to giving teachings from a high throne, surrounded by many monks, and so on, there was a genuine humility. He had no hesitation when it came to doing a chore like emptying the potty of an elderly lady.

~

~

There are particular ways in which one can practice viewing oneself as lower than others. To take a simple example, we all know from experience that when we focus on a particular object or individual, according to the angle from which we view it, we will have a different perspective. This is, in fact, the nature of thought. Thoughts are capable of selecting only isolated characteristics of a given object at a particular time, human thought is not capable of comprehensively viewing something in its entirety. The nature of thought is to be selective. When you realize this, you can view yourself as lower than others from a certain point of view, even in comparison to a tiny insect.

~

Let's say that I compare myself to an insect. I am a follower of the Buddha, and a human being equipped with the capacity to think and, supposedly, to be able to judge between right and wrong. I am also supposed to have some knowledge of the fundamental teachings of the Buddha, and theoretically I am committed to these practices. Yet when I find certain negative tendencies arising in me, or when I carry out negative actions on the basis of these impulses, then from that point of view there is certainly a case to be made that I am in some ways inferior to the insect. After all, an insect is not able to judge between right and wrong in the way humans can, it has no capacity to

~

think in a long-term way and is unable to understand the intricacies of spiritual teachings, so
from the Buddhist point of view, whatever an
insect does is the result of habituation and karma.
By comparison, human beings have the ability
to determine what they do. If, despite this, we
act negatively then it could be argued that we are
inferior to that innocent insect! So when you
think along these lines, there are genuine
grounds for seeing ourselves as inferior to all
other sentient beings.

~

~

The third verse reads:

In all my deeds may I probe into my mind,
And as soon as mental and emotional afflictions arise –
As they endanger myself and others –
May I strongly confront them and avert them.

This indicates that although all of us, as spiritual practitioners, wish to overcome our negative impulses, thoughts and emotions, owing to our long habituation to negative tendencies, and to our lack of diligence in applying the necessary antidotes to them, afflictive emotions and thoughts do occur in us spontaneously and quite powerfully.

~

Such is their force, in fact, that we are often driven by these negative tendencies. This verse suggests we should be aware of this fact so that we remain alert. We should constantly check ourselves and take note when negative tendencies arise in us, so that we can catch them as they arise. If we do this then we will not give in to them; we will be able to remain on our guard and keep a certain distance from them. In this way we won't reinforce them, and we will be spared from undergoing an explosion of strong emotion and the negative words and actions to which that leads.

~

~

But generally, this is not what happens. Even if we know that negative emotions are destructive, if they are not very intense we tend to think, 'Oh, maybe this one is OK.' We tend to treat them rather casually. The problem is that the longer you are accustomed to the afflictions within you, the more prone you become to their reoccurring, and then the greater your propensity will be to give in to them. This is how negativity perpetuates itself. So it is important to be mindful, as the text urges, so that whenever afflictive emotions arise you are able to confront them and avert them immediately.

~

~

It is very important, especially for a Buddhist practitioner, to constantly check oneself in daily life, to
check one's thoughts and feelings even, if possible,
during one's dreams. As you train yourself in the
application of mindfulness, gradually you will be
able to apply it more and more regularly, and its
effectiveness as a tool will increase.

~

~

The next verse reads:

When I see beings of unpleasant character
Oppressed by strong negativity and suffering,
May I hold them dear – for they are rare to find –
As if I have discovered a jewel treasure!

This verse refers to the special case of relating to people who are socially marginalized, perhaps because of their behavior, their appearance, their destitution, or on account of some illness. Whoever practices bodhichitta must take special care of these people, as if, on meeting them, you have found a real treasure. Instead of feeling repulsed,

~

a true practitioner of these altruistic principles should engage and take on the challenge of relating. In fact, the way we interact with people of this kind could give a great impetus to our spiritual practice.

~

~

I am glad to say that I've heard that some Buddhist centers are beginning to apply Buddhist principles socially. For example, I have heard of Buddhist centers involved in some form of spiritual education in prisons, where they give talks and offer counseling. I think this is a great example. It is of course deeply unfortunate when such people, particularly prisoners, feel rejected by society. Not only is it deeply painful for them, but also, from a broader point of view, it is a loss for society. We are not providing the opportunity for these people to make a constructive social contribution when they actually have the potential to do so. I therefore think it is important for society as a whole not to

~

reject such individuals, but to embrace them and acknowledge the potential contribution they can make. In this way they will feel they have a place in society, and will begin to think that they might perhaps have something to offer.

~

~

The next verse reads:

When others, out of jealously
Treat me wrongly with abuse, slander, and scorn,
May I take upon myself the defeat
And offer to others the victory.

The point that is made here is that when others
provoke you, perhaps for no reason or unjustly,
instead of reacting in a negative way, as a true
practitioner of altruism you should be able to be
tolerant towards them. You should remain unper-
turbed by such treatment. In the next verse we
learn that not only should we be tolerant of such

~

people, but in fact we should view them as our spiritual teachers. It reads:

~

~

When someone whom I have helped,

Or in whom I have placed great hopes,

Mistreats me in extremely hurtful ways,

May I regard him still as my precious teacher.

In Shantideva's *Guide to the Bodhisattva's Way of Life*, there is an extensive discussion of how we can develop this kind of attitude, and how we can actually learn to see those who perpetrate harm on us as objects of spiritual learning. And also, in the third chapter of Chandrakirti's *Entry to the Middle Way*, there are profoundly inspiring and effective teachings on the cultivation of patience and tolerance.

~

The seventh verse summarizes all the practices that we have been discussing. It reads:

In brief, may I offer benefit and joy
To all my mothers, both directly and indirectly,
May I quietly take upon myself
All hurts and pains of my mothers.

This verse presents a specific Buddhist practice known as 'the practice of giving and taking' (*tong len*), and it is by means of the visualization of giving and taking that we practice equalizing and exchanging ourselves with others.

~

~

'Exchanging ourselves with others' should not be taken in the literal sense of turning oneself into the other and the other into oneself. This is impossible anyway. What is meant here is a reversal of the attitudes one normally has towards oneself and others. We tend to relate to this so-called 'self' as a precious core at the center of our being, something that is really worth taking care of, to the extent that we are willing to overlook the well-being of others. In contrast, our attitude towards others often resembles indifference; at best we may have some concern for them, but even this may simply remain at the level of a feeling or an emotion. On the whole we are indifferent towards

~

others' well-being and do not take it seriously. So the point of this particular practice is to reverse this attitude so that we reduce the intensity of our grasping and the attachment we have to ourselves, and endeavor to consider the well-being of others as significant and important.

~

~

When approaching Buddhist practices of this kind, where there is a suggestion that we should take harm and suffering upon ourselves, I think it is vital to consider them carefully and appreciate them in their proper context. What is actually being suggested here is that if, in the process of following your spiritual path and learning to think about the welfare of others, you are led to take on certain hardships or even suffering, then you should be totally prepared for this. The texts do not imply that you should hate yourself, or be harsh on yourself, or somehow wish misery upon yourself in a masochistic way. It is important to know that this is not the meaning.

~

Another example we should not misinterpret is the verse in a famous Tibetan text which reads, 'May I have the courage if necessary to spend aeons and aeons, innumerable lifetimes, even in the deepest hell realm.' The point that is being made here is that the level of your courage should be such that if this is required of you as part of the process of working for others' well-being, then you should have the willingness and commitment to accept it.

~

~

A correct understanding of these passages is very important, because otherwise you may use them to reinforce any feelings of self-hatred, thinking that if the self is the embodiment of self-centeredness, one should banish oneself into oblivion. Do not forget that ultimately the motivation behind wishing to follow a spiritual path is to attain supreme happiness, so just as one seeks happiness for oneself one is also seeking happiness for others. Even from a practical point of view, for someone to develop genuine compassion towards others, first he or she must have a basis upon which to cultivate compassion, and that basis is the ability to connect to one's own feelings and to care for one's

~

own welfare. If one is not capable of doing that, how can one reach out to others and feel concern for them? Caring for others requires caring for oneself. The practice of *tong len*, giving and taking, encapsulates the practices of loving-kindness and compassion: the practice of giving emphasizes the practice of loving-kindness, whereas the practice of taking emphasizes the practice of compassion.

~

~

Shantideva suggests an interesting way of doing this practice in his *Guide to the Bodhisattva's Way of Life*. It is a visualization to help us appreciate the shortcomings of self-centeredness, and provide us with methods to confront it. On one side you visualize your own normal self, the self that is totally impervious to others' well-being and an embodiment of self-centeredness. This is the self that only cares about its own well-being, to the extent that it is often willing to exploit others quite arrogantly to reach its own ends. Then, on the other side, you visualize a group of beings who are suffering, with no protection and no refuge. You can focus your attention on specific individuals if

~

you wish. For example, if you wish to visualize someone you know well and care about, and who is suffering, then you can take that person as a specific object of your visualization and do the entire practice of giving and taking in relation to him or her. Thirdly, you view yourself as a neutral third person or impartial observer, who tries to assess whose interest is more important here. Isolating yourself in the position of neutral observer makes it easier for you to see the limitations of self-centeredness, and realize how much fairer and more rational it is to concern yourself with the welfare of other sentient beings.

~

~

As a result of this visualization, you slowly begin to feel an affinity with others and a deep empathy with their suffering, and at this point you can begin the actual meditation of giving and taking.

~

~

In order to carry out the meditation on taking, it is often quite helpful to do another visualization. First, you focus your attention on suffering beings, and try to develop and intensify your compassion towards them, to the point where you feel that their suffering is almost unbearable. At the same time, however, you realize that there is not much you can do to help them in a practical sense. So in order to train yourself to become more effective, with a compassionate motivation you visualize taking upon yourself their suffering, the causes of their suffering, their negative thoughts and emotions, and so forth. You can do this by imagining all their suffering and negativity as a stream of

~

dark smoke, and you visualize this smoke dissolving into you. In the context of this practice you can also visualize sharing your own positive qualities with others. You can think of any meritorious actions that you have done, any positive potential that may lie in you, and also any spiritual knowledge or insight that you may have attained. You send them out to other sentient beings, so that they too can enjoy their benefits. You can do this by imagining your qualities in the form of either a bright light or a whitish stream of light, which penetrates other beings and is absorbed into them. This is how to practice the visualization of taking and giving.

~

Of course, this kind of meditation will not have a material effect on others because it is a visualization, but what it can do is help increase your concern for others and your empathy with their suffering, while also helping to reduce the power of your self-centeredness. These are the benefits of the practice. This is how you train your mind to cultivate the altruistic aspiration to help other sentient beings. When this arises together with the aspiration to attain full enlightenment, then you have realized bodhichitta, that is, the altruistic intention to become fully enlightened for the sake of all sentient beings.

~

~

In the final verse, we read:

May all this remain undefiled
By the stains of the eight mundane concerns;
And may I, recognizing all things as illusion,
Devoid of clinging, be released from bondage.

The first two lines of this verse are very critical for a genuine practitioner. The eight mundane concerns are attitudes that tend to dominate our lives generally. They are: becoming elated when someone praises you, becoming depressed when someone insults or belittles you, feeling happy when you experience success, being depressed

~

when you experience failure, being joyful when you acquire wealth, feeling dispirited when you become poor, being pleased when you have fame, and feeling depressed when you lack recognition.

~

~

A true practitioner should ensure that his or her cultivation of altruism is not defiled by these thoughts. For example, if, as I am giving this talk, I have even the slightest thought in the back of my mind that I hope people admire me, then that indicates that my motivation is defiled by mundane considerations, or what the Tibetans call the 'eight mundane concerns.' It is very important to check oneself and ensure that is not the case. Similarly, a practitioner may apply altruistic ideals in his daily life, but if all of a sudden he feels proud about it and thinks, 'Ah, I'm a great practitioner,' immediately the eight mundane concerns defile his practice. The same applies if a practitioner thinks,

~

'I hope people admire what I'm doing,' expecting to receive praise for the great effort he is making. All these are mundane concerns that spoil one's practice, and it is important to ensure that this does not happen so we keep our practice pure.

~

~

As you can see, the instructions that you can find in the *lo-jong* teachings on transforming the mind are very powerful. They really make you think. For example there is a passage which says:

May I be gladdened when someone belittles me, and may I not take pleasure when someone praises me. If I do take pleasure in praise then it immediately increases my arrogance, pride, and conceit; whereas if I take pleasure in criticism, then at least it will open my eyes to my own shortcomings.

This is indeed a powerful sentiment.

~

~

Up to this point we have discussed all the practices that are related to the cultivation of what is known as 'conventional bodhichitta,' the altruistic intention to become fully enlightened for the benefit of all sentient beings. Now, the last two lines of the Eight Verses relate to the practice of cultivating what is known as 'ultimate bodhichitta,' which refers to the development of insight into the ultimate nature of reality. Although the generation of wisdom is part of the bodhisattva ideal, as embodied in the six perfections, generally speaking, as we saw earlier, there are two main aspects to the Buddhist path – method and wisdom. Both are included in the definition of enlightenment, which

~

is the non-duality of perfected form and perfected wisdom. The practice of wisdom or insight correlates with the perfection of wisdom, while the practice of skillful means or methods correlates with the perfection of form.

~

~

The Buddhist path is presented within a general framework of what are called Ground, Path, and Fruition. First, we develop an understanding of the basic nature of reality in terms of two levels of reality, the conventional truth and the ultimate truth; this is the ground. Then, on the actual path, we gradually embody meditation and spiritual practice as a whole in terms of method and wisdom. The final fruition of one's spiritual path takes place in terms of the non-duality of perfected form and perfected wisdom.

~

~

The last two lines read:

And may I, recognizing all things as illusion,
Devoid of clinging, be released from bondage.

These lines actually point to the practice of cultivating insight into the nature of reality, but on
the surface they seem to denote a way of relating
to the world during the stages of post-meditation.
In the Buddhist teachings on the ultimate nature
of reality, two significant time periods are distin-
guished; one is the actual meditative session
during which you remain in single-pointed meditation, and the other is the period subsequent to

the meditative session when you engage actively with the real world, as it were. So, here, these two lines directly concern the way of relating to the world in the aftermath of one's meditation. This is why the text speaks of appreciating the illusion-like nature of reality, because this is the way one perceives things when one arises from single-pointed meditation.

~

~

In my view, these lines make a very important point because sometimes people have the idea that what really matters is single-pointed meditation within the meditative session. They pay much less attention to how this experience should be applied in post-meditation periods. However, I think the post-meditation period is very important. The whole point of meditating on the ultimate nature of reality is to ensure that you are not fooled by appearances, and that you appreciate the gap between how things appear to you and how they really are. Buddhism explains that appearances can often be deluding. With a deeper understanding of reality, you can go beyond appearances

~

and relate to the world in a much more appropriate, effective, and realistic manner.

~

~

I often give the example of how we should relate to our neighbors. Imagine that you are living in a particular part of town where interaction with your neighbors is almost impossible, and yet it is actually better if you do interact with them rather than ignore them. To do so in the wisest way depends on how well you understand your neighbors' personality. If, for example, the man living next door is very resourceful, then being friendly and communicating with him will be to your benefit. At the same time, if you know that deep down he can also be quite tricky, that knowledge is invaluable if you are to maintain a cordial relationship and be vigilant so that he does not take

~

advantage of you. Likewise, once you have a deeper understanding of the nature of reality, then in post-meditation, when you actually engage with the world, you will relate to people and things in a much more appropriate and realistic manner.

~

~

THE EIGHT VERSES ON TRANSFORMING THE MIND

With a determination to achieve the highest aim

For the benefit of all sentient beings,

Which surpasses even the wish-fulfilling gem,

May I hold them dear at all times.

Whenever I interact with someone,

May I view myself as the lowest amongst all,

And, from the very depths of my heart,

Respectfully hold others as superior.

~

In all my deeds may I probe into my mind,

And as soon as mental and emotional afflictions arise –

As they endanger myself and others –

May I strongly confront them and avert them.

When I see beings of unpleasant character

Oppressed by strong negativity and suffering,

May I hold them dear – for they are rare to find –

As if I have discovered a jewel treasure!

When others, out of jealously

Treat me wrongly with abuse, slander, and scorn,

May I take upon myself the defeat

And offer to others the victory.

~

When someone whom I have helped,

Or in whom I have placed great hopes,

Mistreats me in extremely hurtful ways,

May I regard him still as my precious teacher.

In brief, may I offer benefit and joy

To all my mothers, both directly and indirectly,

May I quietly take upon myself

All hurts and pains of my mothers.

May all this remain undefiled

By the stains of the eight mundane concerns;

And may I, recognizing all things as illusion,

Devoid of clinging, be released from bondage.

~

GENERATING THE MIND
FOR ENLIGHTENMENT

For those who admire the spiritual ideals of the Eight Verses on Transforming the Mind it is helpful to recite the following verses for generating the mind for enlightenment. Practicing Buddhists should recite the verses and reflect upon the meaning of the words, while trying to enhance their altruism and compassion. Those of you who are practitioners of other religious traditions can draw from your own spiritual teachings, and try to commit yourselves to cultivating altruistic thoughts in pursuit of the altruistic ideal.

~

With a wish to free all beings
I shall always go for refuge
to the Buddha, Dharma and Sangha
until I reach full enlightenment.

Enthused by wisdom and compassion,
today in the Buddha's presence
I generate the Mind for Full Awakening
for the benefit of all sentient beings.

As long as space endures,
as long as sentient beings remain,
until then, may I too remain
and dispel the miseries of the world.

~

In conclusion, those who, like myself, consider themselves to be followers of Buddha, should practice as much as we can. To followers of other religious traditions, I would like to say, 'Please practice your own religion seriously and sincerely.' And to non-believers, I request you to try to be warm-hearted. I ask this of you because these mental attitudes actually bring us happiness. As I have mentioned before, taking care of others actually benefits you.

Continuing on this path, you will also begin to appreciate the value of human life, how precious it is, and the fact that as human beings we are capable of reflecting on these questions and

~

following a spiritual practice. Then you will really appreciate a point emphasized again and again by many great Tibetan masters: that we should not waste the opportunity offered to us in this life, because human life is so precious and so difficult to achieve. As life is valuable it is important to do something meaningful with it right now, since, by its very nature, it is also transient. This shows how you can bring all the elements of the various spiritual practices together so that they have a cumulative effect on your daily practice.

~

PART NINE

COMPASSION –
THE BASIS FOR HUMAN
HAPPINESS

~

I think that every human being has an innate sense of "I." We cannot explain why that feeling is there, but it is. Along with it comes a desire for happiness and a wish to overcome suffering. This is quite justified: we have a natural right to achieve as much happiness as possible, and we also have the right to overcome suffering.

~

~

The whole of human history has developed on the basis of this feeling. In fact it is not limited to human beings; from the Buddhist point of view, even the tiniest insect has this feeling and, according to its capacity, is trying to gain some happiness and avoid unhappy situations.

~

~

However, there are some major differences between human beings and other animal species. They stem from human intelligence. On account of our intelligence, we are much more advanced and have a greater capacity. We are able to think much farther into the future, and our memory is powerful enough to take us back many years. Furthermore, we have oral and written traditions which remind us of events many centuries ago. Now, thanks to scientific methods, we can even examine events which occurred millions of years ago.

~

~

So our intelligence makes us very smart, but at the same time, precisely because of that fact, we also have more doubts and suspicions, and hence more fears. I think the imagination of fear is much more developed in humans than in other animals. In addition, the many conflicts within the human family and within one's own family, not to mention the conflicts within the community and between nations, as well as the internal conflicts within the individual – all conflicts and contradictions arise from the different ideas and views our intelligence brings. So unfortunately, intelligence can some-times create a quite unhappy state of mind. In this sense, it becomes another source of human misery.

~

Yet, at the same time, I think that, ultimately, intelligence is the tool with which we can overcome all these conflicts and differences.

~

~

From this point of view, of all the various species of animal on the planet, human beings are the biggest troublemakers. That is clear. I imagine that if there were no longer any humans on the planet, the planet itself would be safer! Certainly millions of fish, chicken, and other small animals might enjoy some sort of genuine liberation!

~

~

It is therefore important that human intelligence be utilized in a constructive way. That is the key. If we utilize its capacity properly, then not only human beings would become less harmful to each other, and to the planet, but also individual human beings would be happier in themselves. It is in our hands. Whether we utilize our intelligence in the right way or the wrong way is up to us. Nobody can impose their values on us. How can we learn to use our capacity constructively? First, we need to recognize our nature and then, if we have the determination, there is a real possibility of transforming the human heart.

~

~

On this basis, I will speak on how a human being can find happiness as an individual, because I believe the individual is the key to all the rest. For change to happen in any community, the initiative must come from the individual. If the individual can become a good, calm, peaceful person, this automatically brings a positive atmosphere to the family around him or her. When parents are warm-hearted, peaceful and calm people, generally speaking their children will also develop that attitude and behavior.

~

~

The way our attitude works is such that it is often troubled by outside factors, so one side of the issue is to eliminate the existence of trouble around you. The environment, meaning the surrounding situation, is a very important factor for establishing a happy frame of mind. However, even more important is the other side of the issue, which is one's own mental attitude.

~

~

The surrounding situation may not be so friendly, it may even be hostile, but if your inner mental attitude is right, then the situation will not disturb your inner peace. On the other hand, if your attitude is not right, then even if you are surrounded by good friends and the best facilities, you cannot be happy. This is why mental attitude is more important than external conditions. Despite this, it seems to me that many people are more concerned about their external conditions, and neglect the inner attitude of mind. I suggest that we should pay more attention to our inner qualities.

~

~

There are a number of qualities which are important for mental peace, but from the little experience I have, I believe that one of the most important
factors is human compassion and affection: a sense
of caring.

~

~

Let me explain what we mean by compassion. Usually, our concept of compassion or love refers to the feeling of closeness we have with our friends and loved ones. Sometimes compassion also carries a sense of pity. This is wrong – any love or compassion which entails looking down on the other is not genuine compassion. To be genuine, compassion must be based on respect for the other, and on the realization that others have the right to be happy and overcome suffering just as much as you. On this basis, since you can see that others are suffering, you develop a genuine sense of concern for them.

~

~

As for the closeness we feel toward our friends,
this is usually more like attachment than compassion. Genuine compassion should be unbiased.
If we only feel close to our friends, and not to
our enemies, or to the countless people who are
unknown to us personally and toward whom
we are indifferent, then our compassion is only
partial or biased.

~

~

As I mentioned before, genuine compassion is based on the recognition that others have the right to happiness just like yourself, and therefore even your enemy is a human being with the same wish for happiness as you, and the same right to happiness as you. A sense of concern developed on this basis is what we call compassion; it extends to everyone, irrespective of whether the person's attitude toward you is hostile or friendly.

~

~

One aspect of this kind of compassion is a sense of caring responsibility. When we develop that kind of motivation, our self-confidence increases automatically. This in turn reduces fear, and that serves as a basis for determination. If you are really determined right from the beginning to accomplish a difficult task, then even if you fail first time, second time, third time, it doesn't matter. Your aim is very clear, so you will continue to make an effort. This sort of optimistic and determined attitude is a key factor for success.

~

~

Compassion also brings us an inner strength. Once it is developed, it naturally opens an inner door, through which we can communicate with fellow human beings, and even other sentient beings, with ease, and heart to heart. On the other hand, if you feel hatred and ill-feeling toward others, they may feel similarly toward you, and as a result suspicion and fear will create a distance between you and make communication difficult. You will then feel lonely and isolated. Not all members of your community will have similar negative feelings toward you, but some may look on you negatively because of your own feeling.

~

∼

If you harbor negative feelings toward others, and yet expect them to be friendly to you, you are being illogical. If you want the atmosphere around you to be more friendly, you must first create the basis for that. Whether the response of others is positive or negative, you must first create the ground of friendliness. If others still respond to you negatively after this, then you have the right to act accordingly.

∼

~

I always try to create a ground of friendliness with people. Whenever I meet someone new, for example, I feel no need for introductions. The person is obviously another human being. Maybe sometime in the future, technological advances may mean that I could confuse a robot for a human being, but up to now this has never happened. I see a smile, some teeth and eyes, and so on, and I recognize the person as a human being! On that basis, on the emotional level we are the same, and basically on the physical level we are the same, except for coloring. But whether Westerners have yellow hair, or blue hair, or white hair, does not really matter. The important thing is that we are the

~

same on the emotional level. With that conviction, I feel that the other person is a human brother, and approach him spontaneously. In most cases, the other person immediately responds accordingly, and becomes a friend. Sometimes I fail, and then I have the liberty to react according to the circumstances.

~

~

Basically, therefore, we should approach others openly, recognizing each person as another human being just like ourselves. There is not so much difference between us all.

~

~

Compassion naturally creates a positive atmosphere, and as a result you feel peaceful and content. Wherever there lives a compassionate person, there is always a pleasant atmosphere. Even dogs and birds approach the person easily. Almost fifty years ago, I used to keep some birds in the Norbulingka Summer Palace, in Lhasa. Among them was a small parrot. At that time I had an elderly attendant whose appearance was somewhat unfriendly – he had very round, stern eyes – but he was always feeding this parrot with nuts and so on. So whenever the attendant would appear, just the sound of his footsteps or his coughing would mean the parrot would show some excitement.

~

The attendant had an extraordinarily friendly manner with that small bird, and the parrot also had an amazing response to him. On a few occasions I fed him some nuts but he never showed such friendliness to me, so I started to poke him with a stick, hoping he might react differently; the result was totally negative. I was using more force than the bird had, so it reacted accordingly.

~

~

Therefore, if you want a genuine friend, first you must create a positive atmosphere around you. We are social animals, after all, and friends are very important. How can you bring a smile to people's faces? If you remain stony and suspicious, it is very difficult. Perhaps if you have power or money, some people may offer you an artificial smile, but a genuine smile will only come from compassion.

~

~

The question is how to develop compassion. In fact, can we really develop unbiased compassion at all? My answer is that we definitely can. I believe that human nature is gentle and compassionate, although many people, in the past and now, think that it is basically aggressive. Let us examine this point.

~

At the time of conception, and while we are in our mother's womb, our mother's compassionate and peaceful mental state is a very positive factor for our development. If the mother's mind is very agitated, it is harmful for us. And that is just the beginning of life! Even the parents' state of mind at conception is important. If a child is conceived through rape, for example, then it will be unwanted, which is a terrible thing. For conception to take place properly, it should come from genuine love and mutual respect, not just mad passion. It is not enough to have some casual love affair, the two partners should know each other well and respect each other as people; this is the basis

~

for a happy marriage. Furthermore, marriage itself should be for life, or at least should be long lasting. Life should properly start from such a situation.

~

~

Then, according to medical science, in the few weeks after birth, the child's brain is still growing. During that period, the experts claim that physical touch is a crucial factor for the proper development of the brain. This alone shows that the mere growth of our body requires another's affection.

~

~

After birth, one of the first acts on the mother's side is to give milk, and from the child's side it is to suckle. Milk is often considered a symbol of compassion. Without it, traditionally the child cannot survive. Through the process of suckling there comes a closeness between mother and child. If that closeness is not there, then the child will not seek its mother's breast, and if the mother is feeling dislike toward the child her milk may not come freely. So milk comes with affection. This means that the first act of our life, that of taking milk, is a symbol of affection.

~

~

It has been found that those children who grow up in homes where there is love and affection have a healthier physical development and study better at school. Conversely, those who lack human affection have more difficulty in developing physically and mentally. These children also find it difficult to show affection when they grow up, which is such a great tragedy.

~

~

Now let us look at the last moment of our lives –
death. Even at the time of death, although the
dying person can no longer benefit much from
his friends, if he is surrounded by friends his
mind may be more calm. Therefore throughout
our lives, from the very beginning right up to our
death, human affection plays a very important
role.

~

～

An affectionate disposition not only makes the mind more peaceful and calm, but it affects our body in a positive way too. On the other hand, hatred, jealousy and fear upset our peace of mind, make us agitated and affect our body adversely. Even our body needs peace of mind, and is not suited to agitation. This shows that an appreciation of peace of mind is in our blood.

～

~

Therefore, although some may disagree, I feel that although the aggressive side of our nature is part of life, the dominant force of life is human affection. This is why it is possible to strengthen that basic goodness which is our human nature.

~

~

We can also approach the importance of compassion through intelligent reasoning. If I help another person, and show concern for him or her, then I myself will benefit from that. However, if I harm others, eventually I will be in trouble. I often joke, half sincerely and half seriously, saying that if we wish to be truly selfish then we should be wisely selfish rather than foolishly selfish. Our intelligence can help to adjust our attitude in this respect. If we use it well, we can gain insight as to how we can fulfill our own self-interest by leading a compassionate way of life.

~

~

In this context, I do not think that selfishness is wrong. Loving oneself is crucial. If we do not love ourselves, how can we love others? It seems that when some people talk of compassion, they have the notion that it entails a total disregard for one's own interests – a sacrificing of one's interests. This is not the case. In fact genuine love should first be directed at oneself.

~

~

There are two different senses of self. One has no hesitation in harming other people, and that is negative and leads to trouble. The other is based on determination, willpower, and self-confidence, and that sense of "I" is very necessary. Without it, how can we develop the confidence we need to carry out any task in life? Similarly, there are two types of desire also. However, hatred is invariably negative and destructive of harmony.

~

~

How can we reduce hatred? Hatred is usually pre-ceded by anger. Anger rises as a reactive emotion, and gradually develops into a feeling of hatred. The skillful approach here is first to know that anger is negative. Often people think that as anger is part of us, it is better to express it, but I think this is mis-guided. You may have grievances or resentment due to your past, and by expressing your anger you might be able to finish with them. That is very possi-ble. Usually, however, it is better to check your anger, and then gradually, year by year, it diminishes. In my experience, this works best when you adopt the position that anger is negative and it is better not to feel it. That position itself will make a difference.

~

Whenever anger is about to come, you can train yourself to see the object of your anger in a different light. Any person or circumstance which causes anger is basically relative; seen from one angle it makes you angry, but seen from another perspective you may discover some good things in it. We lost our country, for example, and became refugees. If we look at our situation from that angle, we might feel frustration and sadness, yet the same event has created new opportunities – meeting with other people from different religious traditions, and so on. Developing a more flexible way of seeing things helps us cultivate a more balanced mental attitude. This is one method.

~

There are other situations where you might fall sick, for example, and the more you think about your sickness the worse your frustration becomes. In such a case, it is very helpful to compare your situation with the worst case scenario related to your illness, or with what would have happened if you had caught an even more serious illness, and so on. In this way, you can console yourself by realizing that it could have been much worse. Here again, you train yourself to see the relativity of your situation. If you compare it with something that is much worse, this will immediately reduce your frustration.

~

Similarly, if difficulties come they may appear enormous when you look at them closely, but if you approach the same problem from a wider perspective, it appears smaller. With these methods, and by developing a larger outlook, you can reduce your frustration whenever you face problems. You can see that constant effort is needed, but if you apply it in this way, then the angry side of you will diminish. Meanwhile, you strengthen your compassionate side and increase your good potential. By combining these two approaches, a negative person can be transformed into a kind one.

~

~

In addition, if you have religious faith, it can be useful in extending these qualities. For example, the Gospels teach us to turn the other cheek, which clearly shows the practice of tolerance. For me, the main message of the Gospels is love for our fellow human beings, and the reason we should develop this is because we love God. I understand this in the sense of having infinite love. Such religious teachings are very powerful to increase and extend our good qualities. The Buddhist approach presents a very clear method. First, we try to consider all sentient beings as equal. Then we consider that the lives of all beings are just as precious as our own, and through this we develop a sense of concern for others.

~

~

What of the case of someone who has no religious faith? Whether we follow a religion or not is a matter of individual right. It is possible to manage without religion, and in some cases it may make life simpler! But when you no longer have any interest in religion, you should not neglect the value of good human qualities. As long as we are human beings, and members of human society, we need human compassion. Without that, you cannot be happy. Since we all want to be happy, and to have a happy family and friends, we have to develop compassion and affection. It is important to recognize that there are two levels of spirituality, one with religious faith, and one without.

~

With the latter, we simply try to be a warm-hearted person.

~

~

We should also remember that once we cultivate a compassionate attitude, non-violence comes automatically. Non-violence is not a diplomatic word, it is compassion in action. If you have hatred in your heart, then very often your actions will be violent, whereas if you have compassion in your heart, your actions will be non-violent.

~

~

As I said earlier, as long as human beings remain on this Earth there will always be disagreements and conflicting views. We can take that as given. If we use violence in order to reduce disagreements and conflict, then we must expect violence every day and I think the result of this is terrible. Furthermore, it is actually impossible to eliminate disagreements through violence. Violence only brings even more resentment and dissatisfaction.

~

~

Non-violence, on the other hand, means dialogue, it means using language to communicate. And dialogue means compromise: listening to others' views, and respecting others' rights, in a spirit of reconciliation. Nobody will be a 100 percent winner, and nobody will be a 100 percent loser. That is the practical way. In fact, that is the only way. Today, as the world becomes smaller and smaller, the concept of "us" and "them" is almost out-dated. If our interests existed independently of those of others, then it would be possible to have a complete winner and a complete loser, but since in reality we all depend on one another, our interests and those of others are very interconnected. So how can you gain a 100 percent victory? It is impossible. You have to share, half-half, or maybe 60 percent this side and 40 percent the other side! Without this approach, reconciliation is impossible.

~

The reality of the world today means that we need to learn to think in this way. This is the basis of my own approach – the "middle way" approach. Tibetans will not be able to gain 100 percent victory because whether we like it or not, the future of Tibet very much depends on China. Therefore, in the spirit of reconciliation, I advocate a sharing of interests so that genuine progress is possible. Compromise is the only way. Through non-violent means we can share views, feelings, and rights, and in this way we can solve the problem.

~

~

I sometimes call the 20th century a century of bloodshed, a century of war. Over this century there have been more conflicts, more bloodshed, and more weapons than ever before. Now, on the basis of the experience we have all had in this century, and of what we have learned from it, I think we should look to the next century to be one of dialogue. The principle of non-violence should be practiced everywhere. This cannot be achieved simply by sitting here and praying. It means work and effort, and yet more effort.

~

PART TEN

QUESTIONS AND
ANSWERS

~

Your Holiness, in this modern world, we try to avoid suffering. This only seems to create more suffering in that one person's positive work can be someone else's suffering, for instance medicine, politics, and so on. How do we judge? Shouldn't we just accept a certain amount of suffering and discomfort?

~

~

I think that there are many levels of suffering. Generally speaking, it is definitely possible to reduce the level of suffering. I don't personally believe that conditions that are essential for one's wellbeing and happiness necessarily involve harming and affecting someone else's life in a negative way.

Here I would like to say something. I feel that television and newspapers usually report negative things. Killings, for example, or unfortunate events are immediately reported. In the meantime, millions of people are actually receiving help, or being nourished or looked after by human affection, such as millions of children,

~

sick and old people. But usually in people's minds these good things are taken for granted. They are not seen as something to which we should pay special attention. Actually, this shows that the very nature of humanity is compassion or affection. We simply ignore all the work of affection because it seems natural. But we are surprised at things like bloodshed; it shocks our minds because our nature is not of that kind.

As a result, many people get the impression that human nature is negative, aggressive, and violent. I think that psychologically this is very bad, especially for young children who, through television, see negative human elements, but

~

always for a short time. At that moment or for a short period, these things like killing or hitting can be a little bit exciting. But in the long-term, I think these violent things are very, very harmful to society. In fact, I recently had a meeting with Karl Popper, the philosopher. We have known each other since 1973. In our meeting we discussed violence on television and my view that too much violence is having a very negative impact on the minds of millions of children. He is, I think, of the same opinion. A proper way of education is the most important element in terms of hope for a better future.

~

~

Your Holiness, what is your answer on how to stop pollution in the universe? Will there have to be an end of the universe and mankind as we know them in order to cleanse and begin again?

~

~

Of course, from the Buddhist viewpoint, not just from that of common sense, there is a beginning and there is an end. That is logical; that is law; that is nature. So whatever we call the Big Bang or such things, there is a process of evolution or a process of beginning. So there must be an end. In any case, I think the end won't come for several million years.

Now, pollution. As you know I come from Tibet. When we were in Tibet, we had no idea about pollution. Things were very clean! In fact, when I first came across pollution and heard people say that I could not drink the water, it was a surprise to me. Eventually our knowledge widened.

~

Now it is really a very serious issue. It is not a question of one nation or two nations, but of the survival and health of all of humanity. If we have a clear conscience about this problem and behave accordingly, it seems there is a way to at least lessen this problem. For example, two or three years ago when I was in Stockholm beside the big river, some of my friends told me that 10 years previously there had been no fish in the river because the water was so polluted. Around the time of my visit some fish had begun to appear because of the control of pollution. So this shows that there is the possibility of improving things.

~

Killing and situations like Bosnia are immediately striking to our minds. Yet pollution and other environmental problems lack this kind of striking appearance. Gradually, month by month, year by year, things become worse and worse. By the time a problem becomes very obvious it may be too late. Therefore I think it is a very serious matter. I am quite encouraged that in many places people are clearly concerned, and even some political parties have been set up based on the ideology and policy of environmental protection. I think this is a very healthy development. So there is hope.

~

~

What suggestions can you offer to overcome social institutions, such as the news, entertainment, and media, which seem constantly to promote negative attitudes and emotions – the opposite of what you advocate?

~

~

That is true. I often express my concern at that. However, I think, as we discussed, much depends on our own mental attitude. When we look at these negative things – killing, sex, or that kind of thing – if we look at them from another angle, that is also useful. Sometimes you can use these scenes of violence, sex, and so forth in a more positive way, so that, by being mindful of the effect and destructive nature of these various human emotions, you can use this particular viewing as a reminder of their destructive nature. While images of sex and violence may be some-what exciting initially, if you look further you can see no benefit.

~

Of course, I have another opinion of the media, I think especially in the West. In a country like India, killing and murder are often shown on television, but the sexual things are more censored. But if you compare killing and sex, sex is much better! If we pretend that it is not a part of human life, that is also not good, is it?

Anyway, I think it is equally important to make a clear presentation to the human mind of the other, good, human qualities, and I think that this is lacking. We only show the negative side – killing, sex, and all these things – but the other side, the human acts of compassion, are not shown.

~

Now, for example, in Washington I visited the museum of the Holocaust. When I went there, after seeing all these things, I was reminded of both qualities of human beings. On the one side there was Nazi Germany's torture, killing, and extermination of the Jewish people – horrible and very sad. It reminds me how bad or awful it is if human intelligence is guided or motivated by hatred. But at the same time, another side showed those people who sacrificed their own lives in order to protect Jewish people. So that also shows the human good quality, to risk even their own lives to save unfortunate people. In that way, I think it was quite balanced. If we let hatred guide

~

us then we can be so cruel and so destructive. But on the other hand, if we promote good human qualities, then wonderful actions and marvelous things can happen. Likewise, the media should show both sides. That is what I always feel.

~

~

Your Holiness, racism, bigotry and human folly seem to be on the increase. To what negative factors do you ascribe this? What positive factors can combat this trend?

~

~

I think they largely depend on education. I feel that the more correct information and the more awareness and contact you have, the better. Of course, you also have to adopt an open mind. After all, you are just one human being out of five billion and one individual's future depends very much on others. Part of the problem I see is a lack of awareness of other cultures and the existence of other communities, and also a lack of understanding of the nature or reality of modern existence. If it were possible to gain complete satisfaction and fulfilment by being totally independent within one's own culture and one's own community – to be totally independent and unrelated to other

~

communities around the world – then perhaps one could argue that there were grounds for subscribing to these misconceptions like bigotry and racism. But this is not the case. The reality of the existence of other cultures and other communities cannot be ignored. Moreover, the nature of modern existence is such that the well-being, happiness and success of one's own community are very connected with the well-being and interests of other communities and other societies. In such a complex modern world there is no room for bigotry and racism.

Now according to my own experience, there is no doubt that Buddhism is the most suitable

~

religion for me. But this does not mean that Buddhism is best for everyone. Each individual has a different mental disposition and therefore for some people a particular religion is more suitable or more effective than others. So if I respect each individual's right, then I must respect or accept the value of these different religions because they work for millions of other people.

When I was in Tibet I had little information, through books or from personal contact, about the nature and value of other traditions. Since I've become a refugee, I have had more opportunity to have closer contact with other traditions, mainly through individuals, and I have gained a much deeper understanding of their value. As a result, my attitude now is that each one is a valid religion. Of course, even from the philosophical viewpoint, I still believe that Buddhist philosophy is more sophisticated, that it has more variety or is more vast, but all other religions still have tremendous benefits or great potential. So on both bases, I think my attitude towards other religions is greatly changed. Today, wherever I go and whenever I meet someone who follows a different religion, I deeply admire their practice and I very sincerely respect their tradition.

~

Is it possible for an ordinary person to transform his or her fear and despair? How can we do this?

~

~

Oh, yes, it is very possible. For example, when I was young I was always afraid of dark rooms. As time went by, the fear went. Also, with regard to meeting people, the more your mind is closed, the greater the possibility of developing fear or feeling uncomfortable. The more open you are, the less uncomfortable you will feel. That is my experience. If I meet anyone, whether a great man, a beggar, or just an ordinary person, to me there is no difference. The most important thing is to smile and to show a genuine human face. Different religions, different cultures, different languages, different races – these are not important. Educated or uneducated, rich or poor, there is

~

no difference. When I open my heart and open my mind, I consider people just like old friends. This is very useful. On the basis of that kind of attitude, if the situation is something different then I have the freedom to act according to the circumstances. But at the beginning, from my side, I must create the ground. Then often there is a positive response from the human level. So I think fear is one thing to clear away.

~

~

Also, in the individual's mind there are many hopes. If one hope fails, it does not mean that all hopes fail. I have met some people who tend to feel completely overwhelmed and who become desperate when they are not able to fulfill one of their hopes. But I believe that the human mind is very complex. We have so many different types of hopes and fears that it is quite dangerous to invest everything on one particular hope, so that when that hope is not fulfilled we are totally overwhelmed. That is a bit too dangerous.

~

Your Holiness, in this country there has been a move away from religion in recent years. At the same time, there has been an increased interest in various forms of self-development. Is religion still an appropriate path in the modern world?

~

It is definitely relevant in the modern world. But perhaps I should clarify this. Many years have passed since various religious traditions started, so certain aspects are, I think, perhaps out of date. But this does not mean that religion as a whole is irrelevant in modern times. Therefore, it is important to look at the essence of the different religions, including Buddhism. Human beings, no matter whether today's or those of 100, 1,000, 4,000 or 5,000 years ago, are basically the same. Of course, a lot of the cultures and the ways of life have changed, but still we have the same kind of human being. So therefore, the basic human problems and suffering – such as death, old age, disease, fighting and

~

all these things – are still there. I don't know what kind of shape humans will be in after 10,000 years or 100,000 years; nobody knows. But at least over the last few thousand years, they have, I think, kept basically the same nature.

So I think the various different religions actually deal with basic human suffering and problems. On that level, because human nature and suffering have remained the same, the religions are still very relevant. On the other hand, certain ceremonial aspects and so on have changed. In India, during the feudal system or the reign of kings, the way of practice was very much influenced by those circumstances. But that has changed and, I think, has to change further.

~

As far as Buddhism is concerned, it of course not only deals with this life but with other more mysterious aspects. Unless, just as modernization is taking place in our world, a similar type of modernization is taking place in other realms of existence, I think Buddhism will retain its relevance and appropriateness, not only to our modern world, because many of the fundamental problems of human existence still remain, but also because it addresses issues which are related to other mysterious forms of existence. I always believe that the modern change is just a surface change and that deep down we are the same. Last year at the border between Austria and Italy, they recovered an old

~

body. If we were to suppose that the person was alive, I think we could still communicate with him. Yet the body is about 4,000 years old. Of course, that person would have a different culture and maybe a slightly different way of expression, but basically we could still communicate.

~

*Could Your Holiness speak about interpersonal rela-
tionships in accordance with personal karma? How
does one understand the difference between tolerance and stupidity?*

~

True tolerance is a stand or a response an individual adopts in relation to a particular incident, or toward another person or event, when the individual has the ability to act in a contrary manner. As a result of one's considerations, taking into account many factors and so on, the individual decides against taking negative action, and this is true tolerance. This is quite different from a situation in which an individual has no capacity whatsoever to take such a strong countermeasure. Then he or she is in a helpless position, so can't do otherwise. The difference between the two is in fact quite clearly pointed out in one of the Buddhist texts known as *Compendium of Deeds*

~

by the Indian master Shantideva. So my tolerance toward the Chinese is actually quite open to question – is it really genuine tolerance or not?!

~

~

How may one overcome fear or fearfulness as a habitual state of mind, especially when there is no apparent cause?

~

~

I think that the kind of outlook you have and the way you think makes a big difference. Often we find ourselves being hit by a sudden thought or feeling, such as fear, which, if we leave to itself, or, in other words, give in to without paying much attention, can begin to work in its own cause and begin to affect us. It is crucial that when such things arise one must apply one's faculty of reasoning so that one does not fall under the sway of these thoughts and feelings. Of course, if there is sufficient reason to fear, then fear is good! Fear creates preventive measures, so that's good. Yet if there is no basis for fear, then when you meditate analytically the fear will be reduced. That's the proper way.

~

Can compassion arise spontaneously after one has developed direct intuitive insight?

~

~

I think it depends very much upon one's own spiritual orientation and the basic motivation. It is possible for certain practitioners who have developed familiarity with various principles of the path, altruism, and so forth. As the individual gains greater insight into the nature of reality, the greater the power of his or her compassion and altruism will be, because he or she will then see that sentient beings revolve in the cycle of existence due to ignorance of the nature of reality. Such practitioners, when they gain very deep insight into the nature of reality, will also realize the possibility of a way out from that state of suffering. Once you have that realization, then your compassion toward sentient beings will be greater because then you will realize their fate – although they can get out, they are still caught in the cycle.

But simply because one has gained a certain degree of insight into the nature of reality does not guarantee an automatic spontaneous experience of compassion. This is because one's insight into the nature of reality can be motivated by an altruistic wish to help other sentient beings or it can be induced by a motivation primarily concerned with one's own interest of attaining liberation from cyclic existence. So simply by generating insight into the nature of reality on its

~

own cannot really lead to genuine compassion;
you need some additional conditions.

~

~

Are there examples of the positive expression of anger based on compassion and self-understanding?

~

~

Yes, it is possible to have circumstances in which the basic motivation can be compassionate, but the immediate catalyst or motivating factor can be anger, which is a very strong force of mind.

~

~

Your Holiness, how can I stay in touch with my emotions without being afraid? I often control my feelings so much that I am closed off and unable to love.

~

~

When I talk about love and compassion, I make distinctions between the ordinary sense of love and what I mean by love. What I mean by love can arise on the basis of a clear recognition of the existence of the other person, and a genuine respect for the wellbeing and rights of others. However, love based on strong attachment toward one's close ones is, from the point of view of religious practice, something that has to be ultimately purified. A certain degree of detachment must be developed.

~

~

I think that perhaps at the beginning level you may find some kind of loneliness. Actually, that is one of the aims of the lives of monks and nuns. While in one way that sort of life may seem a bit colorless or unattractive, in another way it is more colorful. In reality, I think the one form of happiness has too much fluctuation, so I think in the long run the other type, although less dramatic, is something steady. In the long run I think that it is much more comfortable! So that is one consolation for monks and nuns!

~

~

If someone feels in the depths of despair and, in a very deep depression, lies at night wanting to die, what is your advice to help that person become more stable and positive?

~

~

It is very difficult if it is someone who has no background or practice. Then I really don't know what to advise. But if it is someone who has some experience or practice of some other religion, and if he or she has some experience of Buddhist practice, then it is helpful to think about Buddha Nature and about the potential of the human body and the human brain. It is also helpful to read the stories of great practitioners of the past, whose lives illustrate the hardships that people have gone through. For instance, in some cases these great masters were people who had previously had almost no education or people who were depressed and lacked facilities and so forth. But as a result

~

of their determination and confidence in their own potential, they were eventually able to attain high realizations. One must also bear in mind that being depressed and losing hope will never really help to correct the situation.

~

~

Your Holiness, in trying to be a compassionate human being, how responsible should we feel? What should you do if you find someone emotionally dependent on your compassion? Is it compassionate to hurt someone if you think it is the best in the long run?

~

~

I think you should keep in mind compassion with wisdom. It is very important to utilize one's faculty of intelligence to judge the long-term and short-term consequences of one's actions.

~

~

I can understand how my own mind and actions can affect my own causes and conditions. Can they also affect world conditions like hunger, poverty, and other great sufferings of beings everywhere? How?

~

~

Sometimes we feel that one individual's action is very insignificant. Then we think, of course, that effects should come from channeling or from a unifying movement. But the movement of the society, community or group of people means joining individuals. Society means a collection of individuals, so the initiative must come from individuals. Unless each individual develops a sense of responsibility, the whole community cannot move. So therefore it is very essential that we should not feel that individual effort is meaningless – you should not feel that way. We should make an effort.

~